Just-Right
Comprehension
Mini-Lessons

GRADES 4–6

CHERYL M. SIGMON
& LISA D. GILPIN

New York • Toronto • London • Auckland • Sydney
Mexico City • New Delhi • Hong Kong • Buenos Aires

Teaching *Resources*

Dedication

To my wonderful husband, Bryan, for always being there for me. This book would not have been possible without your support. I have been blessed to have you as my husband. Thank you for your love, laughter, and encouragement. I also want to thank my parents for always believing in me. Thanks for your love and support —LDG

To my husband, Ray . . . At the end of seven books in this series, I thank you, from the depths of my heart, for understanding my passion and supporting my pursuits in life. For every dream I've ever had, you've encouraged me. What a wonderful life partner you are! —CMS

At the end of a long series of comprehension and writing mini-lesson books, we recognize someone who has been alongside us on this journey, someone who has been loyal, steadfast, and focused on producing the best mini-lesson series possible—Merryl Maleska Wilbur. Merryl, it's been quite a journey indeed as you guided us through metaphoric hailstorms and stick-figured mice, saved us from green eggs on our faces, and, on at least one occasion, proofed lessons while handling a hospital emergency! There's no way to thank you enough for your significant contributions to this series. It's been both a pleasure and a true honor to work with you.

Acknowledgments

Special thanks to Scholastic's Terry Cooper and Virginia Dooley, who had faith in the ability of this series to support teachers and in the authors to write it.
Sincere thanks as well to Chris Borris, who copyedited this complete comprehension series with a thorough eye to detail and true professionalism.

Jennifer Downing, Teacher, Sand Creek Elementary, North Vernon, IN
Patty Ertel, Principal, Sand Creek Elementary School, North Vernon, IN
Sylvia M. Ford, Consultant, Columbia, SC
Staci Gilpin, Future teacher, Cincinnati, OH
Amanda Hite, Teacher, Sand Creek Elementary, North Vernon, IN
Ann Hollar, Consultant, Huntington, IN
Sierra Jackson, Principal, and the teachers of Custer Hill Elementary School, Ft. Riley, KS
Debbi McKinley, Teacher, Sand Creek Elementary, North Vernon, IN
Kristi Morris, Teacher, Sand Creek Elementary, North Vernon, IN
Shelly Neal, Teacher, Northside Elementary School, Hartford City, IN
Leanna Phillippe, Principal, Jac-Cen-Del Elementary School, Osgood, IN
Donata Shockley, Paraprofessional, Sand Creek Elementary, North Vernon, IN
Christa Tolliver, Teacher, Thomas Jefferson Elementary School, Jeffersonville, IN
Dr. Jerry Chabot, Superintendent, Dr. Linda Walker, and the teachers and administrators of Montpelier Elementary, Northside Elementary, and Southside Elementary in the Blackford County School District, Hartford City, IN
Dr. Dave Wall, Assistant Superintendent, Lisa Wiedmann and the principals and teachers of the Rhinelander School System, Rhinelander, WI
Beyond the research that has been cited in this book, gratitude is extended to the teachers who took that research and made it practical and teachable in the classroom. Stephanie Harvey and Ann Goudvis in *Strategies that Work*; Deb Miller's *Reading with Meaning*; Ellin Keene and Susan Zimmerman's *Mosaic of Thought*; and Linda Hoyt's *Reread, Revise, and Revisit*—all give us not only the insight but also the courage to begin our own exploration in the classroom without fearing the unknown.

Cover design and cover photo by Maria Lilja.
Interior design by Holly Grundon.
Interior photos courtesy of the authors.

ISBN-13: 978-0-439-89906-2
ISBN-10: 0-439-89906-0

Table *of* Contents

Section Three: Generating and Answering Questions

Section Four: Using Graphic and Semantic Organizers

Section Five: Creating and Using Images

Section Six: Accessing Prior Knowledge

Section Seven: Summarizing

Section Eight: Using Text Features and Organizers

Appendices

Bibliography

Introduction

The focus of the books in this Just-Right Comprehension series is reading comprehension, which for several decades has been considered the "essence of reading" (Durkin, 1993). We have known for many years now that a child who is word calling well is not necessarily really reading. However, it is a disappointing fact that this knowledge has not translated into successful student achievement in reading comprehension.

It is a matter of grave concern that 36 percent of fourth graders scored below the basic level on the 2005 National Assessment of Educational Progress (NAEP) report card and that 69 percent of fourth graders scored below the proficient level on that same measure. Further disconcerting is the fact that those 2005 scores reflect very little change from the fourth-grade 1992 NAEP scores. These statistics are even more dismal when seen within the context of the Carnegie Report (1995), which informed us that eight million young people in fourth through twelfth grades struggle to read at grade level. This means that about 70 percent of our students in these grades require some kind of remediation because they cannot comprehend what they have read. This is a startling statistic, indeed.

Researchers have looked for causes that might explain this failure of our students to read proficiently. Among the foremost reasons is lack of instruction in reading comprehension strategies— those strategies that can be transferred beyond the immediate text to other situations (Pressley, Wharton-McDonald, et al., 1998; Cunningham, 2007). Although studies have confirmed that classroom time is regularly allotted to both practice and testing of comprehension strategies, they have also revealed an almost total absence of comprehension strategy instruction in our classrooms.

As part of a series that addresses grades 1 to 6, this book aims to help teachers convert solid research into daily instruction. These simple but powerful mini-lessons teach, explicitly and directly, the valuable comprehension strategies that students need. The instruction in this book is based on a model of gradual release of responsibility from the teacher to the learners in the classroom (Pearson and Gallagher, 1983). After modeling and thinking aloud during these lessons, you will guide and monitor students as they apply the same skill or strategy.

Our hope is that these mini-lessons can offer teachers tools and ways of approaching text with students that turn instruction into lifelong lessons to be applied by students far beyond the classroom. With the support of research, we believe that teaching comprehension strategies well can put our students on solid ground as skillful readers for a lifetime. By using these lessons, you should find this critical task far less daunting and far more doable!

CONTEXTS AND FRAMEWORKS FOR DAILY MINI-LESSONS

These mini-lessons are the teacher's opportunity to provide direct instruction in key comprehension skills and strategies that students at grades 4 to 6 need to become good readers. The lessons' great advantage is that they can be implemented in a number of different natural classroom contexts. For example, these mini-lessons will work well within guided reading lessons; reading workshops; tutorial sessions; small group instruction; and content area lessons, in which understanding about how to read and manage text is important. Here's a brief explanation of how they might work within each of these contexts:

- **Guided Reading Lessons** The first segment of a guided reading lesson—the time dedicated to a teacher's modeling what students are expected to do during their own reading—is an ideal instructional home for these mini-lessons. Frequently there is also a step in the mini-lesson outline that describes students' own reading and sometimes one that involves the teacher's closure and summarizing. Thus, in several different ways, you should be able to fold these lessons right into the framework of a guided reading lesson.

- **Reading Workshops** The Reading Workshop begins with a teacher's modeling and demonstrating what a good reader does. These mini-lessons are an ideal launch point for the Workshop because direct instruction and modeling lie at the core of the lessons.

- **Tutorial Sessions** These lessons are ideal for use in tutorial sessions that target specific students' needs. Just use the book's table of contents and the Matrix of Standards to locate a lesson that focuses on a particular skill or strategy needed by a student. Also, because the mini-lessons are written step-by-step in a clearly delineated standard format, they should be accessible to all, including assistants supporting regular classroom teachers.

- **Small-Group Instruction** Just as with Tutorial Sessions, these mini-lessons can drastically cut planning time for teachers who need to design lessons for targeted small-group instruction. Identify the common instructional need of several students and then use the table of contents and the Matrix of Standards to locate the appropriate lesson(s) to teach that skill or strategy.

- **Content Area Lessons** Many of these mini-lessons make use of science or social studies text, thus demonstrating how easy it is to integrate literacy and content instruction. Students need to see how they can use literacy skills to help them make sense of content area information and communicate it to others.

HOW THESE MINI-LESSONS FIT WITHIN THE OVERALL SERIES

The challenges for upper-grade students include navigating increasingly complex informational text and engaging in more sophisticated, higher-level thinking skills.

From the very start—print and language basics in the first-grade book that quickly move to lessons on navigating simple narrative and expository text—this series has always stressed the goal of readers' making meaning. In the book for grades 2 to 3, students quickly move from instruction in basics of fluency development and decoding strategies to greater challenges. The focus on narrative text shifts to teaching students to analyze, rather than to simply identify, literary elements. In addition, reflecting a curriculum at these grades that is increasingly content laden, all sections of the book for grades 2 to 3 emphasize the internal and external structure of informational text.

Although it continues to reinforce essential basics such as fluency and word development, this book for grades 4 to 6 is tailored to the needs and interests of upper-grade students. The sections all include lessons that call on more sophisticated, higher-level thinking skills. Students are challenged to analyze, interpret, evaluate, and synthesize and to respond in a variety of innovative ways to their reading.

This book maintains and further develops a key focus of the entire series—the instruction of metacognitive skills. Metacognition, or the ability to think about one's own thinking, involves activities like purposefully planning for reading, making and confirming predictions, and self-monitoring understanding. It has proven to be the critical factor in students' success as reflected by previous research on both the fourth and eighth grade NAEP tests (Wenglinsky, 2004). Because metacognition is increasingly needed in the more challenging texts that upper-grade students confront, we have treated it as an underpinning for all these lessons.

We imagine that teachers willing and ready to use this book are like us in at least one critical way: They find it unacceptable that so many of our students fail to connect what they have learned to new situations or to act effectively on that knowledge (Bransford, Franks, Vye, & Sherwood, 1989). Our greatest hope for these lessons is that they will enable young readers to take what they know and transfer it to the other reading they do—whether on tests, in content reading, or in the reading they do in their everyday lives.

Standards

Along with the National Standards, the standards of the following ten states were gathered to create the curriculum for this book: California, Colorado, Florida, Indiana, New York, Pennsylvania, South Carolina, Texas, Virginia, and Washington.

HOW THESE MINI-LESSONS WERE DEVELOPED

The curriculum for the lessons in this book is based on a number of documents. As a first step in developing the lessons, we looked into whether educators around the United States generally hold common beliefs about what students need to know and do in reading comprehension in fourth through sixth grades. We selected ten states that represent different geographical regions as well as diverse populations and studied the standards documents for these states. Not surprisingly, we found a high correlation of commonalities among the documents. Some terminology differed, but the basic thinking was similar. Across the country, it seems that we have pretty much agreed about what constitutes good reading among our students in fourth through sixth grades.

Next, we studied another important and widely regarded document, *The National Reading Panel Report* (2000), to find out how its experts regard reading comprehension and whether its beliefs are congruent with the states' beliefs. We discovered that while the standards/objectives defined by the states were more discrete and specific than the broader strategies identified in the national document, the two sources corroborated each other and were highly compatible.

Indeed, the two sources work hand-in-hand extremely well. The states' standards can be seen as the focused guidelines necessary to help students achieve the broader, more general strategies suggested by the National Reading Panel. Therefore, in organizing this book and developing the lessons, we used the national strategies as the basis for the section divisions and the more discrete standards as the springboards for the lessons themselves.

THE NATURE OF A GOOD MINI-LESSON

An effective reading comprehension mini-lesson is direct and explicit and focused solely on the targeted comprehension skill or strategy. Lessons shouldn't confuse the students by introducing grammar, mechanics, usage, long- and short-vowel sounds, digraphs, and similar skills. There are other opportunities in the instructional day when these skills can best be taught and understood. Reserve your mini-lesson exclusively for those skills and strategies that have direct impact on the meaning derived from reading text.

There is another key aspect to the effective mini-lesson: While direct and explicit, mini-lesson instruction does not simply tell students what they need to know. Instead, it involves a teacher's active,

In an effective mini-lesson a teacher clearly defines the targeted strategy and actively demonstrates it for students.

dynamic modeling of the targeted skill and/or strategy. Modeling the thinking and the decisions that a reader must make, even the little ones, will allow these same thought processes to become part of your students' habits. Thus, a critical part of your modeling is "thinking aloud," or expressing aloud the process you are following as you read a piece of text and apply a strategy or utilize a skill. Many students, especially beginning readers, don't know how to actively reflect as they read. Your demonstrating how to do this becomes a key part of your students' development as readers.

Two Approaches

Here are two mini-lessons that show a clear difference in their approach to instruction. Let's peek into the classrooms below to compare the effectiveness of the two different lessons.

Teacher A

In this sixth-grade classroom, the students are beginning to read a novel, *Freak the Mighty* by Rodman Philbrick. Their reading of this novel will span a period of several weeks. Understanding the need to set a purpose for reading, Teacher A has posted a list of questions on the board for students to answer upon completion of their reading that day. The questions include: Who are the main characters? How old are they? What appeals to each of these boys about the other? To be sure that students understand what the questions mean, the teacher reads each question aloud and discusses it. He then sets a timer and assigns the students to small groups. As the students read, they stop occasionally when they realize they have an answer to one of the questions written on the board. They make note of it and then continue with their reading. The teacher monitors the progress of the groups and reminds them of the time. After reading is concluded, he brings the class together so that they can share the answers to the posted questions.

Teacher B

In her classroom, Teacher B begins a lesson based on the same novel by posing a question about friendship—What makes a good friend? She asks students in small groups to turn to one another and discuss this question for a few minutes. She then reveals the book's cover and title. She reminds students that even though she wants them to enjoy the novel, she also wants this to be an opportunity to apply new and old comprehension strategies. "In this lesson I'm going to demonstrate what you'll be doing today that will help you enjoy this story and, more importantly, that will make you a better overall reader," she explains. Then she reads aloud the first two pages. Maxwell talks about sizing up his young friends. At this point, the teacher pauses and says, "I think this is believable. I remember doing this, too. In my first-grade class, there was a biter and a crier. That's the way we thought of each other." Then she adds, "These are connections I'm making between the book and my own experiences in life. It's the way we gain better understanding of what we read." She challenges students to make their own connections to what they read and tells them to jot down their connections on sticky notes to place on the text. Students delve into the novel to get the job done.

At the closure of a well-constructed lesson, you'll likely find students better prepared to answer a most important question. Read on to find out exactly what the question is.

DID THE LESSON SUCCEED?

A great aid to teachers in analyzing the success of reading lessons is asking the simple question: *What did my students learn today that will make them better readers?* And you can make this question even more powerful by asking it directly of students themselves. You may be surprised to hear what your students have to say!

If, in answer to this question, students begin to retell what they've read, they have probably not grown much as readers from the lesson. The students in Teacher A's classroom would be more likely to retell the story or to feel that coming up with the precise answers to the posted questions was the point of the lesson. The lesson has several basic shortcomings: Most critically, because it doesn't define a real instructional goal nor actively demonstrate application of skills, there is likely to be little or no transfer from the lesson to students' real reading.

In Teacher B's classroom, on the other hand, the reason for reading and the expectation that the lesson be transferred are both clear. The teacher states that she wants the students to enjoy the novel and, more importantly, that she wants them to use the lesson as an opportunity to apply skills and strategies that will make them better readers. She also clearly defines the targeted strategy and goes on to actively demonstrate it. When asked the important question of how the lesson will make them better readers, these students should be able to say in their own words that making connections between the text and one's own life helps a reader to make better sense of the text. If students are able to articulate what they have learned about a lesson's skill or strategy, there's a greater likelihood that they'll take that skill and use it when it counts—in their real reading

HOW TO USE THIS BOOK

INSTRUCTIONAL FLEXIBILITY

If your school uses a basal reader program for instruction, there are several ways to organize your year using the lessons in this book. You might follow your basal curriculum and consult the Table of Contents in this book to find a lesson to help you teach the skill/strategy the basal curriculum calls for. Or, you might follow this book, and then use your basal as it meets the text criteria specified for each lesson.

If your school's approach is literature based, you can follow your local curriculum and consult the Table of Contents in this book to see which lesson correlates with the defined skill/strategy. Or, you can follow this book and use your literature for the context of the lessons, again using the text specifications provided in each lesson to locate appropriate material. This book also encourages you to use available content texts, including textbooks, so that students will become comfortable with expository text. This is especially important in grades 4 to 6 because the curriculum is so content-oriented.

It's worth noting that most lessons combine several different standards and target a variety of related skills and strategies. This is only natural because rarely, if ever, can one comprehension strategy be totally isolated from the use and application of other skills and strategies. This kind of mixing and combining offers you further flexibility in picking and choosing to meet the needs of your own students and your curriculum goals.

No matter how you use this book within your overall reading instruction, it's important to take your local or state curriculum and cross-check it with the Table of Contents to see if any gaps exist. You'll also be the best person to make the decision about how often a skill or strategy needs to be revisited and reinforced.

SEQUENCING YOUR LESSONS

For the most part, you can pick and choose lessons randomly throughout the book. We recommend viewing the sections as a menu. You can select lessons appropriately based on your students' needs and on opportunities to integrate lessons with other content being taught.

One exception to your selection of lessons without regard to their sequence in this book is that some lessons are set up purposely in a certain sequence. These are clearly identified as having multiple parts from the start. It's best to look out ahead of time for these lessons so that you won't wind up getting the cart before the horse with activities or with presentation of concepts.

ADDITIONAL CONSIDERATIONS

There are a few additional key considerations to keep in mind as you approach these lessons and as you consider the best ways you will use them within your overall reading curriculum. Below is a list of some of these considerations:

- What printed text should be used? Many of these lessons suggest specific titles, but also provide general guidelines to allow you the freedom to choose what you want to use and to take into consideration the materials that are available in your own teaching situation.

- Is there any vocabulary essential to understanding the printed text you'll be using for a given lesson? You'll want to keep the presentation of vocabulary to a minimum within the context of these mini-lessons, but some words may be critical to preview for students.

- How much support will students need to read the text for a given lesson? Even if a lesson suggests reading the text aloud to your class, you are definitely the best person to decide if a different presentation is called for. Perhaps, for certain lessons and in certain situations, you'll want your students to read chorally with you or with a partner or a small group.

- What will tomorrow's lesson be? You'll base this to a great extent on the closure from the day's lesson and on feedback from previous lessons. If at the conclusion of a lesson you see that your students "got it" and don't need any clarification, then perhaps you'll choose to focus on another skill or strategy the following day. Or perhaps you'll feel they need a little more—or occasionally a lot more—practice, in which case you'll continue to teach and reteach the current skill or strategy. It's all based on students' needs and the evidence you're able to gather.

- The final point is perhaps the most obvious, but it's too often overlooked in the face of all the other demands confronting teachers, so we feel it's worth underscoring. As you plan each lesson, it's clarifying to ask one simple question of yourself: *What do I need to teach that will help my students become better readers?* A direct answer to that question alone would eliminate many lessons presently taught in our classrooms. Too often we teach lessons that are ends in themselves. The text isn't what it's about at all—it's really about how to read the text. What we need to teach are lessons that become the means to achieve more long-range goals for our students as readers. It is the hope and intent of this book to meet that need.

CONSTRUCTING TOOL KITS

Have you noticed some students in your classroom who can sit quietly, perhaps squirming just a bit, for the full duration of a read-aloud? Surely, you've noticed those others—the ones who tend to be always in motion. They drum their fingers on the desk, chew their pencils, shake their legs, or twist and turn in their seats. These kinesthetic learners actually need to move to learn. And, as many of us can attest—this isn't a condition that changes as these students leave the primary grades and move to fourth through sixth grades!

Every classroom includes students at both ends of this spectrum, as well as those in the middle. The lessons in this book promote instruction that taps the different learning styles of all students. You'll find that most lessons offer students the opportunity to be not only mentally engaged in reading but physically/tactilely engaged as well. Something as simple as having students place sticky notes on certain pages or using a highlighter can help focus energy and attention. So we've structured these lessons to include a great deal of students' active involvement. Even those students who don't need this extra element to remain engaged in learning can benefit from and enjoy this kind of dynamic interaction with text.

To make these kinds of activities manageable in the classroom, you may want to create simple kits to help maximize the time your students have to devote to their tasks. Your students will love having their very own tool kits, and you'll love seeing how engaged they become as they put the kits to use. To construct the kits, you'll first need a sealable sandwich bag for each student in the classroom. You can easily personalize these bags by printing your students' names on self-adhesive mailing labels and sticking them to the bags. The tools should be introduced gradually so that students are taught the appropriate use of each and so that the tools won't be overwhelming to them in the beginning. (See page 13 for an illustration of one student's tool kit.)

Here are a few tools that you might choose among for your students' kits:

- **Sticky Notes** About 12 on a pad per kit will be sufficient for a few lessons.

- **VIP Strips** These are sticky notes that you pre-cut, snipping several times toward the sticky end to form "fingers" that students can tear off as needed to mark text. "VIP" stands for Very Important Points (Hoyt, 1999).

- **Glitter Sticks** These are ice-pop sticks or tongue depressors with tips dipped in glue and then in a pretty glitter. Each student needs only one of these for—among many possible uses—identifying vocabulary words and underscoring text clues.

- **Sticky Sticks** These come in packs and look similar to pipe cleaners but have a waxy coating that adheres to book pages. They can cling to a book page and then be stripped away without leaving a residue. They are malleable and also can be cut into smaller strips. They are used to highlight and identify words, phrases, and clues.

- **Pocket Chart Highlighters** These are brightly colored, transparent, flexible plastic strips, approximately 2 inches by 4 inches. They come in packs of about 24 and are useful for highlighting sections of text.

- **Highlighter Pens** These come in a variety of colors and are used to highlight text.

- **Paper Clips** These can be used to flag a page and/or the location on that page of a word or clue that the reader needs to recall.

- **Bookmarks** These can be handy as placeholders and can serve double duty to track print or highlight sentences that are discussed. Bookmarks can be purchased, downloaded free from the Internet, or made by students.

- **Index Cards** Each student's tool kit contains one index card with the word *Yes* and another with the word *No*. These are useful in eliciting responses from all students, thereby helping circumvent the frequent classroom phenomenon in which a few students always respond while others remain passive. When you ask a question, all students are to respond with one of the cards. Include several blank index cards as well. These can be used for many purposes, such as students' written responses to questions.

- **Crayons** A crayon or two can be included for use as highlighters to mark text and for occasional additional uses.

- **Word Frame** For this, you'll use a die-cut template to cut an appealing shape from construction paper. After the figure is cut, snip a small window in the figure. (You might need to fold the figure to make an evenly cut window.) Then, run the figure through your laminator and trim the edges. The result is a fun figure with a window for students to frame words and phrases. See right for one example.

You may think of other items to include in the kits as the year progresses. Have fun creating these kits and guiding your students to use them to get more hands-on involved in reading!

BEYOND THESE LESSONS

We must do two things in addition to teaching the skills and strategies in this book so that students will realize that reading is both a necessary and a joyful part of daily life.

First, we must continue to show students the "real-world" purposes served by reading and being literate. That means bringing in real-world reading materials to share and making those available to the students—take-out menus, classified ads, driver's manuals, nutrition pamphlets, television schedules, how-to manuals, dental hygiene and health care pamphlets, recipe books, newspapers, bus schedules, thank-you notes from relatives and friends, postcards we've received, e-mail messages from teachers in other parts of the country, and many other real-world types of written communication. Students need to see clearly that reading is necessary in our everyday lives.

Students' motivation to read often grows when they are given opportunities to read real-world materials, like magazines.

Second, we need to read aloud to students every single day so that they discover the real joy of reading. Read to them often without any lessons connected—just for pure enjoyment. Let them hear the different sounds and patterns of language and the stories and information that will challenge their minds and imaginations. Engage them in discussions that make reading relevant to their lives. As Jim Trelease (1995) sums it up in *The Read-Aloud Handbook*, "Every time we read to a child, we're sending a 'pleasure' message to the child's brain. You could even call it a commercial, conditioning the child to associate books and print with pleasure."

We hope that this book will help you to accomplish these ambitious goals. Good luck and enjoy!

Matrix of Standards*

Standards	Lesson Page
Follow multi-step directions	All lessons
Use word origins to determine meaning of unknown words	20, 23, 28
Apply knowledge of synonyms, antonyms, homonyms, homographs, and multiple-meaning words to determine meaning of words and phrases	21, 23
Determine meaning of words and phrases using context clues	20, 21, 25, 28, 67
Develop vocabulary through meaningful experiences	22, 82
Use reference aids—thesauruses, atlases, dictionaries, the Internet, glossaries, tables of contents, indexes—effectively and appropriately	22, 55, 82, 88, 104
Make and understand simple and complex analogies	84
Use the meanings of roots, prefixes, and suffixes to determine the meaning of unknown words	22, 28
Generate and answer questions to aid comprehension	42, 45, 46, 48, 49, 50, 52, 53
Use the organization of informational text—comparison-contrast, listing, cause and effect, description, and sequential order—to improve comprehension	63, 109
Use the organizational patterns of narrative text—foreshadowing, flashback, plot within a plot, chronological order	112, 114
Use graphic organizers—concept, hierarchical, cyclical, sequential, matrix—to show organization of the text	22, 32, 33, 34, 38, 40, 52, 55, 61, 63, 64, 69, 70, 72, 75, 115
Make predictions about text	20, 42, 52, 53, 55, 68, 75, 77, 78, 79, 82, 88
Use prior knowledge to aid in comprehension of text	35, 36, 37, 52, 75, 77, 78, 79, 80, 82, 83, 84
Make connections: text-to-self, text-to-text, and/or text-to-world	35, 36, 37, 42, 77, 78, 79, 80, 82, 83, 84
Use text features—headings, subheadings, illustrations, titles, topic sentences, and important words—to predict and monitor comprehension	88, 104, 110, 111
Differentiate between fact and opinion	40
Skim and scan for information	34, 38, 40, 45, 46, 48, 49, 50, 96, 98, 102, 104
Determine and clarify main ideas and details	41, 42, 52, 58, 59, 61, 64, 67, 75, 88, 91, 94, 96, 98, 100, 102, 104
Paraphrase and summarize using main ideas, events, details, and themes	32, 33, 34, 38, 58, 59, 63, 64, 88, 89, 91, 94, 96, 98, 99, 100, 102, 104, 110, 111
Generalize, draw conclusions, and make inferences	33, 42, 88

Identify and analyze the author's purpose	55, 99
Analyze, compare, and contrast themes from a variety of texts	99, 115
Read aloud with fluency, accuracy, and expression	24, 25
Adjust reading rate according to type of text	24, 25
Establish purpose for reading	25, 45, 46, 48, 49, 50, 52, 53, 54
Explain effects of figurative language (simile, metaphor, idiom), symbolism, and imagery in a variety of texts	67, 68, 69, 70, 71, 72
Apply self-monitoring strategies: rereading, summarizing, coding, self-correcting, questioning, discussing	21, 24, 28, 32, 33, 34, 35, 36, 37, 38, 40, 41, 42, 54, 59, 61, 63, 67, 68, 69, 77, 78, 79, 80, 82, 89, 99, 100, 114
Identify characteristics of poetry, as well as narrative, expository, technical, and persuasive text	32, 33, 34, 107, 115
Create mental images to aid comprehension	34, 36, 67, 68, 69, 70, 71, 72
Identify differences among various forms of fiction, including fables, fantasies, historical fiction, legends, myths, and fairy tales	115, 117
Identify main events of the plot	58, 61, 64, 89, 99
Identify and analyze situation, setting, character traits, motives, and cause for characters' actions to determine character traits	32, 33, 34
Compare and contrast story settings, characters, events, and/or ideas; compare and contrast tales from different cultures	64
Identify speaker/point of view and determine whether it is first person or third person	54
Identify elements of poetry: rhyme, tone, form, alliteration, refrain, and stanza	107
Identify conflicts	41
Clarify by use of outlines, notes, diagrams, summaries, and reports	34, 59, 61, 63, 96, 98, 100
Distinguish among types of genres—biography, historical fiction, realistic fiction, informational text, poetry—and their characteristics	53, 107, 115, 117
Classify and categorize ideas	34, 46, 48, 49, 50, 55, 58, 91, 94, 100, 102, 115
Respond to text using a variety of formats: drama, writing, and graphic art; respond to text from different perspectives	34, 36, 37, 38, 55, 68, 70, 71, 72, 83, 89
Detect bias, propaganda techniques, stereotypes, and exaggeration	49, 50
Use a variety of media, including the Internet, computer card catalogues, and encyclopedias	55, 88
Use organizational features and electronic sources—headings and numberings, software, the Internet, pull-down menus, keyword searches, and icons—to access information	82, 88, 104

*Along with the National Standards, the standards of the following ten states were gathered to create the curriculum for this book: California, Colorado, Florida, Indiana, New York, Pennsylvania, South Carolina, Texas, Virginia, and Washington.

Building Fluency Skills and Word-Level Knowledge

Because they are basic reading skills and fundamental building blocks, fluency skills and word knowledge can greatly influence a reader's successful understanding of text. Research substantiates that fluency is one of several critical factors necessary for reading comprehension (National Reading Panel Report; NICHHD, 2000) and that "repeated and monitored oral reading improves fluency and overall reading achievement" (National Institute for Literacy, 2007). Realizing that expression, intonation, and rate are inherent in successful reading, teachers often use evaluations of oral fluency to gauge how well students understand text. They consider such factors as:

- Does the student's voice go up and down appropriate to the punctuation marks?

- Does the expression change as a character speaks?

- Does the student's intonation give a clue as to the tone of the text interpreted by the student?

- Does the student realize that reading isn't a race—that faster isn't necessarily better?

As proof of the correlation between fluency and comprehension, a 1995 study sponsored by the United States Department of Education (Pinnell et al., 1995) demonstrates the close association between oral reading fluency and silent reading comprehension. In the study, the fourth graders who were the most fluent readers also demonstrated the highest comprehension levels. The students who read best orally also scored highest in silent reading comprehension. Moreover, every decline in oral reading fluency was marked by a corresponding decline in silent reading comprehension. And those students who struggled most with oral reading, even though they read with a high level of accuracy, also had the most difficulty in reading comprehension (Rasinski, 2003). Evidence such as this establishes a clear connection between fluency and comprehension.

This class is exploring meaningful word parts by posting and referring to a "Nifty 50" word list.

In the lessons in this section, we approach fluency from several different perspectives. We challenge students to pay closer attention to the mechanical clues on the page—commas, end punctuation, and lines—so that they can read with ease. We also provide an authentic context for students in upper grades to rehearse their reading—a practice students of this age often resist. Other lessons in this section address reading and rereading and monitoring students' oral reading.

Like fluency, word-level knowledge has a direct impact on comprehension of text. In fact, a large vocabulary is both predictive and reflective of high reading achievement (NRPR; NICHHD, 2000). In lieu of the traditional practice of memorizing lists of words for spelling and vocabulary tests, the current and effective approach is to teach students how the English language works so that they can read and write with confidence and proficiency at differing levels of text. For example, knowledge of the meanings of prefixes and suffixes gives students a key to unlock the meanings of countless additional words. Likewise, awareness of origins and meanings of root words enables students to make intelligent choices as they navigate text. Dr. John Pikulski (1995) sums it up so well: "It seems almost impossible to overstate the power of words; they literally have changed and will continue to change the course of world history."

One word-knowledge lesson in this section offers students a look at word parts through something near and dear—their own names. In addition, they are invited to "sample" restaurant menus to discover the many influences of other countries on the English language. Other lessons provide experience with homographs—words that have the same spelling but different origins—and exploration of synonyms and antonyms. With these lessons, your students are sure to find interesting tidbits about word origins, word parts, and word meanings. Additionally in this section, students learn different options for figuring out unfamiliar words encountered in text. As with all the mini-lessons in this book, we model the application of these strategies in a careful, direct way so that students will also apply them automatically when they read on their own.

This section on words and fluency takes what has typically been taught in a dry, dull way and engages students in dynamic explorations. Dive in and have fun!

HAVING FUN WITH THE ORIGINS OF NAMES AND WORDS

Explanation

In a sense, it's a shame that we typically pay much less attention to word origins than to their meanings. Words can simply be a lot of fun! And the more students realize this, the more likely they are to want to spend time exploring text. Investigating word origins should be an adventurous journey into foreign lands–as this lesson using food terms and students' names proves!

Skill Focus

Using word origins to determine meanings of unknown words; using context clues to aid comprehension; following multi-step directions; making predictions about text

Materials & Resources

Text

- Assorted menus from local restaurants

- List of food-related words derived from different languages

Other

- 10 index cards for each group

Bonus Ideas

- Invite students to browse *Always in Good Taste* on the www.doe. state.in.us Web site. It provides fascinating background about culinary words, among other kinds of words.

- Create a "Words From Around the World" resource for your classroom–a booklet to which students can add words with interesting origins that they encounter in their independent reading. Keep this in your writing center.

Prior to the Lesson: Assemble a list of interesting culinary words, choosing from among several languages. You might use the source noted in Bonus Ideas or simply use words from the menus you've collected or from your own cookbooks.

(Optional) To make this lesson even more interesting, go to www.behindthename.com, which lists background information about names. Locate your own and your students' names and print out the information in a format that will allow you to easily create sentence strips. (For certain names, you'll need to check the appropriateness of the gender reference. For example, Jordan or Tyler may be masculine or feminine.)

STEPS

1. Explain to students that not only can exploring word origins help readers figure out the meaning of unknown words—it's also just a lot of fun. This lesson has two angles. First, students will have a chance to think about names, what they mean, and where they've come from. Next, they'll get to examine words for all kinds of different foods and to identify the different languages from which these words originate.

2. If you are using the optional Prior to the Lesson step, distribute sentence strips with students' names. If not, simply write a sample name, with its background, on a transparency or the board. Allow class time for discussion of what makes names interesting, how certain names are related to one another, and so on. Following is an example from www.behindthename.com:

   LISA

   Usage: English, German, Swedish

   Pronounced: LEE-sa (English), LEE-zah (German)

   Short form of ELIZABETH or ELISABETH. The name Lisa appears in the name of one of the most famous paintings in the world, the Mona Lisa, the portrait of the wife of Francesco del Giocondo by Leonardo da Vinci.

3. Next, call students' attention to your list of preselected culinary words. Write them on a transparency or the board. An example list follows:

buffet	spaghetti	burrito
café	tortilla	omelet/omelette

4. Challenge students to identify the appropriate languages of origin. You may want to provide a list, in scrambled order, to facilitate choices. (For the above list, the relevant languages are French, Spanish, and Italian.)

5. Set up small groups. Distribute a restaurant menu and about ten index cards to each group. Have groups comb the menus to find as many words as they can that derive from other languages. Direct them to write each word, a brief definition, and its language of origin on an index card. Conclude by bringing the class together and inviting groups to share their discoveries.

SYNONYMS AND ANTONYMS IN ACTION

Explanation

In this lesson, students have a chance to work graphically with the concept of synonyms and antonyms. After this simple review, they are challenged to use reference sources to find antonyms and synonyms for words they've encountered in text.

Skill Focus

Using synonyms, antonyms, homographs, and context clues to aid comprehension; rereading to find details; using reference aids; determining meanings of multiple-meaning words

Materials & Resources

Text

- Multiple copies of a grade-appropriate text that includes synonyms and antonyms

Other

- 1 sheet of paper or a white dry-erase board for each student

- A large assortment of crayons in one color family

- Chart paper; markers

- 10 index cards for each partner pair

- Reference sources such as dictionaries and Internet access

Bonus Ideas

Start a vocabulary jar in your classroom. When students come across an interesting word, have them write the word, along with its definition, on a small piece of paper or sticky note and place it in the jar. At a certain time in the day—for example, as students line up for lunch—you or a designated student can pull a word from the jar and read it to the class.

STEPS

1. Tell the class that today's lesson will focus on words that have opposite meanings—antonyms—and words that have similar meanings—synonyms. You'll start by asking students to demonstrate their understanding of these kinds of words in two different ways that involve drawing.

2. Explain that you'll begin with some easy antonyms. On the board or a transparency, sketch a simple picture. Next to it draw an arrow pointing up. Direct students to draw an antonym of this picture on their whiteboards or sheets of paper and then to hold them up to show you. Because their drawings will reflect an opposite meaning, they should place an arrow pointing down next to their pictures. Here are some basic antonyms you might use: smiley face (frowning face); boy (girl); cloudy (sunny); eyes closed (eyes open).

3. Next, focus on synonyms. Make available a large assortment of crayons in one color family. Invite students to each select a crayon of any hue in this family—for example, for red they might select brick red, burgundy, cherry, coral, cranberry, crimson, pink, rose, ruby, rust, scarlet, or strawberry.

4. Mount a piece of chart paper. Invite students to come forward individually to draw a small heart and shade it in. Afterward, have students take a moment to survey the entire chart. Ask the class how this assortment of colors might relate to the concept of synonyms. Guide them to realize that these colors are all similar, just as synonyms are. In a visual sense, each red shade on the chart is a "synonym" for the others.

5. Tell students that good readers pay close attention to antonyms and synonyms because they know that these words can help their comprehension. Set up partners. Distribute the preselected text and a set of ten index cards to each pair. Have students read the selection through once.

6. Then instruct students to go back through the text to locate five words for which they think there is a synonym and five words for which they think there is an antonym. They should write each word on one side of an index card. Using prior knowledge, computer thesauruses or dictionaries, and/or classroom thesauruses or dictionaries, they are to write a synonym or an antonym on the back and to identify which kind of word it is. Encourage students to write more than one synonym or antonym, if possible. If they can't find an antonym or synonym for the word, they should choose an alternate word.

7. Now have each partner pair find another pair. Have them quiz one another, discuss their findings, and compare how many different words they've come up with.

ROOTING OUT PREFIXES AND SUFFIXES

Explanation

Familiarity with the meanings of prefixes and suffixes—along with the ability to sort out affixes from root words—can greatly aid readers in determining the meanings of unknown words. This lesson invites students to work cooperatively as they explore words with affixes.

Skill Focus

Using roots, prefixes, and suffixes to determine the meaning of words; using reference aids, including electronic sources; developing vocabulary through meaningful experiences

Materials & Resources

Text

- Multiple copies of a grade-appropriate text that includes numerous words with prefixes and suffixes

Other

- Sentence strips
- Sticky sticks cut into fourths (see p. 14)
- Chart paper; markers; glue
- Reference sources such as dictionaries and Internet access
- 3" x 3" sticky notes; scissors

Bonus Ideas

- The charts that result from this lesson will make a wonderful hallway display.
- A terrific Web site for students is www.allwords.com. When they type in a prefix or suffix and click to indicate whether they want to locate words that begin or end with their word part, they will discover a wealth of information.

Prior to the Lesson: From your preselected text, choose ten words that each contain a prefix or a suffix. Write each word on a sentence strip.

STEPS

1. Tell students that many words are composed of a root word and a word part. Explain that if the word part comes at the beginning of the word, we call it a prefix. If it falls at the end, it's called a suffix. Provide an example of each kind of word, as shown below:

   word with prefix: *review*

   word with suffix: *helpless*

2. On the board or a transparency, write the ten words you've selected. Ask students to help you categorize them into two lists: words that contain prefixes and words that contain suffixes. Rewrite the words to reflect these two categories.

3. Distribute the preselected text and sticky sticks, cut into fourths, to each student. Work with students to locate the ten targeted words in the text. Have students use their sticks to underline the words. With your guidance, have students use clues from the text to develop a definition for each word.

4. Now instruct students to read the story and to pay close attention to the underlined words as they read.

5. Then organize students into ten partner pairs and/or several small groups and give each group a sentence strip containing one targeted word. Distribute a sheet of chart paper to each group. Instruct students to divide the paper into fourths by drawing one line down the center of the paper vertically and one across the paper horizontally.

6. Tell each group to position their word in the center of the chart paper, to glue it in place, and then to number the boxes 1–4. On the board or a transparency, write the following directions for each box and have students use dictionaries (either standard or electronic) to fill in the boxes appropriately.

   Box 1: Write the prefix or the suffix and its meaning, and the root word and its meaning.

   Box 2: Write 3–5 other words containing the same prefix or suffix.

   Box 3: Write a sentence that uses one of the words in Box 2.

   Box 4: Draw a picture to illustrate a different word from Box 2.

7. Finally, invite groups to share their words and to use their charts to teach one another what they've learned.

MULTIPLE-MEANING WORDS: MAKING THE RIGHT CHOICES

Explanation

By the upper grades, most students are quite familiar with simple multiple-meaning words. However, the nuances of more complex words used in different contexts can be tricky. The homographs presented in this lesson offer a challenge for even the most discerning reader, but this is a lesson you'll have fun with.

Skill Focus

Determining meanings of multiple-meaning words; using word origins to determine meanings of unknown words

Materials & Resources

Text

- A selection of newspapers and magazines whose headlines you can use to illustrate various homographs

Other

- Sentence strips with homographs

Bonus Ideas

A game of charades is a great way to help students sort through the different meanings of multiple-meaning words. Distribute cards with multiple-meaning words to teams of students. Two teams get the same word but with a different meaning identified on the card. Have one group act out their word and see if the other team with that same word can figure it out. Here is a list of words to get started: *well* (not sick)/*well* (source of water); *fair* (just)/*fair* (event with rides); *mine* (gold)/*mine* (possession); *rose* (flower)/*rose* (past tense of *rise*); and *ground* (dirt)/*ground* (chopped up).

STEPS

1. Alert students that you will start this lesson by writing on the board a word that you want them to pronounce. They'll get only one chance to pronounce it correctly and only three seconds to do it. Write the word *bass* and count aloud to three. Ask students to pronounce the word.

2. Now tell the class that you'll give them a headline for a newspaper article that contains the word in Step 1. They need to decide if they think they pronounced the word correctly. Write on the board:

   Fishing Tournament Breaks All Records

   For this sentence, students should make a connection to bass, the fish. Correctly pronounce the word *bass* for them with a short *a* sound.

3. Now repeat the process in Step 2 with the headline that follows:

   Rock Band Goes on Tour

   For this headline, the correct pronunciation is *bass* with a long *a* sound—as in bass guitar or bass tones. Students should realize that either pronunciation they may have called out originally is correct—it's the context that determines which one is appropriate.

4. Write *homograph* on the board. Explain that *bass/bass* is an example of a homograph, an interesting type of multiple-meaning word. Underline *homo-* and tell students that this word part means "same." Underline *-graph* and explain that it means "written." Together, the word parts in *homograph* mean: "a word that is written, or spelled, the same." Homographs have different meanings, different origins, and often (but not always) different pronunciations. They just happen to be spelled the same way. Good readers use context to help them figure out the correct meaning and pronunciation of a homograph in text.

5. Set up partners or small groups. Distribute a sentence strip with a different homograph to each group. Challenge students to create two different headlines for their homograph, one for each meaning. Afterward, have groups share their headlines. A sample list of homographs follows:

   - **Wind:** word relating to air and word meaning "turn"

   - **Present:** word meaning "gift" and word meaning "here"

   - **Dove:** word for a bird and word that is the past tense of *dive*

   - **Tear:** word relating to crying and word meaning "shred"

   - **Bow:** word meaning "bend at the waist" and word meaning "ornate ribbon"

PAYING ATTENTION TO PUNCTUATION TO IMPROVE FLUENCY

Explanation

Students often read through a selection without paying any attention to punctuation, but heeding punctuation is a crucial element in reading fluently, whether silently or aloud. In this lesson you demonstrate just what readers lose by reading poetry that way. Then students themselves experience what readers can gain by attending to a poem's punctuation.

Skill Focus

Adjusting reading rate according to type of text; reading aloud with fluency/accuracy/expression; rereading to find details and to self-correct; following multi-step directions

Materials & Resources

Text

• Grade-appropriate poem that includes a variety of punctuation marks (. , ? ! : ; -) (Recommended for this lesson: "Messy Room" by Shel Silverstein, from *A Light in the Attic*)

• For students' work: an assortment of such poems

Other

• Transparency of model poem

• Multiple photocopies of poems for students' work

• 5 different-colored transparency markers

• Multiple crayons in same 5 colors

STEPS

1. Tell students that in today's lesson they'll be asked to pay close attention to punctuation in poetry. Punctuation plays a critical role in all text because it directs readers to heed such fundamentals as when to stop, start, or pause. In addition, punctuation guides readers about when to raise or lower their voices and tells them when to read with liveliness. This is especially important in poetry, which is usually meant to be read aloud.

2. Read aloud the preselected poem without paying attention to the punctuation. Challenge students to critique your reading. Ask them if what they heard made sense and was easy to understand.

3. Now display the prepared transparency of your selected poem. At the top of the transparency, add a key, color-coding each punctuation mark differently. A sample key is at right.

Stop : ; .
Pause — ,
Raise your voice ?
Lower your voice .
Read with liveliness !

4. With students' help, work your way through the poem. As you locate each punctuation mark, use an appropriately colored marker to circle it.

5. Now reread the poem to the class, this time paying close attention to the punctuation. Have students compare your two readings.

6. Next, direct students to read the poem chorally (in unison). Tell them to be especially careful to pay attention to each punctuation mark and to let it guide the inflection of their voices as well as their rate and rhythm. Repeat this process as many times as you feel are needed.

7. Tell students it's time for them to try this on their own. Make available an assortment of poems and invite students to read through them to choose one they'd like to practice reading fluently.

8. Distribute crayons. Direct students to circle all the punctuation marks in their poem. They should follow the key displayed on the transparency and use appropriately colored crayons. Once they have marked all punctuation, they are to practice reading the poem quietly or silently to themselves.

9. Finally, place students with partners or in groups and have them read their poems aloud to one another. Circulate around the room, taking anecdotal notes, as needed.

10. Conclude by having the class discuss how they think this lesson will help them in other subject areas. Among other points, guide them to realize that using punctuation in their writing will help better ensure that readers interpret their work appropriately. Invite students to explain why using punctuation correctly helps all readers better comprehend the text.

FLUENCY FOR A PURPOSE

Explanation

In the lower grades, teachers quite often have students read and reread text to develop fluency, with little resistance from their students (who love to hear the same story a hundred times!). In the upper grades, students are less likely to enjoy rereading unless there is a distinct purpose for doing so. This lesson provides an authentic purpose for developing fluency by offering students the opportunity to participate in a service project.

Skill Focus

Reading aloud with fluency/ accuracy/expression; determining meaning of words and phrases using context clues; adjusting reading rate according to type of text; establishing purpose for reading

Materials & Resources

Text

- Any grade-appropriate text that will allow you to demonstrate fluency conventions (Used in this lesson: *Whiz Kid Quarterbacks* by Tom Barnidge)

- An assortment of narrative and expository texts and poetry appropriate for the targeted audience

Other

- Transparency of the portion of the selected text you're using for modeling

- Different-colored highlighters (if student texts are consumable, such as magazines) or sticky notes (for non-consumable texts)

- Recorders and tapes or CDs

Note: Although we have not broken this lesson into parts, it should be considered a multiday lesson.

Prior to the Lesson: Work with other teachers or community members to locate an audience of younger readers or less able students who would benefit from having a store of books on tape available. Possible groups/settings include lower-grade classes, students with special needs, or a nearby day-care facility or children's hospital. If you cannot readily locate such an audience, you can alter the goal of this lesson just slightly: Students can create the tapes for your classroom library so that they, as well as your future students, can make use of them.

STEPS

1. Tell students that you need their help to establish an audio library of books on tape. Identify the audience you've located and explain why students' help is necessary. Their task is to make recordings of selected books for the target audience. Because the tapes will be used in real settings by real children, the books need to be read with excellent expression and correct intonation. The tapes need to sound professional! Doing that will take some work.

2. The first point students need to consider is the genre—informational material, narrative, or poetry—that they'll be reading. Each genre has its own special requirements. Following is a list of tips that you might list on a transparency or chart paper:

How Genre Affects Fluency

- Informational text should be read evenly, much as a television reporter or announcer would do. The text is delivered with fewer high and low pitches than other genres.

- Informational text tends to have less dialogue. When there is dialogue, it too should be read in an even tone.

- Informational text is usually read at a steady rate.

- Narrative text tends to have a good deal of dialogue. The dialogue should be read to sound as if a particular character is actually speaking—much like an actor reading a script and playing a role.

- The tone and rate of narrative reading usually fluctuate widely, according to what is being said or described.

- The pitch of narrative reading—the way a reader's voice goes up and down—should show much expression.

- The way a particular poem should be read greatly depends on the punctuation and varies with the mood and tone of the piece.

Bonus Ideas

- Expose students to many different professional readings so that they can study and critique the various styles. There are a number of good Web sites that provide free audio excerpts of professional readers. Try www.librivox.org --it has professional readings of complete texts that are considered part of the public domain. Among those readings you'll find a number of well-known stories and poetry. You might also consider sites such as www.eyeintheear.com, which offer audio tapes for sale but which provide colorful excerpts of works free of charge.

- Share with your class the wonderful children's book, *Eats, Shoots and Leaves: Why Commas Really Do Make a Difference*, based on the best-selling adult version by a similar name. This book illustrates just how drastically punctuation marks can alter meaning. Students will love it!

3. Display a transparency of the selected text. Mark and discuss cues that will guide your reading. Below is a list of steps you might follow:

   - Underline any difficult words. Look them up in the dictionary to check pronunciations.

   - Highlight punctuation marks that call for voice changes. (Refer to the lesson on punctuation conventions, p. 24.)

   - Highlight words you want to stress with your voice.

4. Now read the selected text aloud and think aloud about the decisions you make as you read. Make a point of demonstrating how you use your voice to express meaning and how you use the punctuation as a guide. A possible think-aloud, based on the sample book, follows:

Sample Text Read Aloud (showing underlining and highlighting teacher might make during the reading)	Teacher's Think-Aloud
Philadelphia fans **booed** on draft day in 1999, when the Eagles used their **first** pick to choose quarterback **Donovan McNabb** from Syracuse University. Eagles fans wanted **their** team to pick **running back** Ricky Williams, who **led** the nation in rushing at the University of Texas. "I didn't take it personally," said McNabb, "but it was **embarrassing** for my mom and dad." Since then, McNabb has changed **jeers** to **cheers** by leading the Eagles to **three playoff berths**...	"I know right away that this is informational text, and I'll be reading it in an even, steady way, just as a TV reporter would do." "I want to be sure to slow down a bit with names that are not familiar to me." "I want to say running back as though it were a compound word. I don't want to split those two words in my reading. It would sound funny." "If *jeers* were a word I didn't know, I would look it up to be sure of its pronunciation. Having the word *cheers* as a rhyming word there helps me. I'm not familiar with the word *berths*, so I'll use the dictionary to have a better understanding."

Bonus Ideas

- Here's a great way to draw attention to the way punctuation is used in text. For a zany Readers Theater, choose an interesting, lively text that includes both considerable dialogue and several different characters. In addition to assigning parts for the characters, assign some students to be punctuation marks. Each child designated as a specific punctuation mark should develop a unique sound for his or her part. For example, if a person is a period, he or she might make a "pow" sound; a comma might be a "zip"; and so on. Students will probably laugh hysterically during the popping, clicking, zipping antics of this theater production!

5. Tell students that you're going to finish reading the story. But first you'll share some criteria for a good read-aloud. You want students to listen carefully to your reading and to use this list to evaluate how you sound. Following is a list of guidelines you might provide:

   My reading will sound fluent if...

   - ... it is smooth rather than choppy.

   - ... my reading rate is appropriate for the type of text.

   - ... I have had adequate practice.

   - ... unfamiliar words were researched and spoken correctly.

   - ... my tone of voice is appropriate for the type of book.

   - ... my pitch changes at the right times.

   - ... my expression is appropriate and interesting.

6. Read the full selection aloud and engage the class in a critique of your reading. Encourage students to refer to all three lists of guidelines you've discussed in the lesson.

7. Make available an assortment of books and poems. Have students each select a story, informational book, or poem(s). Advise them to choose carefully because this will be the basis for their "professional" reading.

8. Set up partners or small groups. Have students use highlighters or sticky notes to mark their texts and then practice reading for their partners or group members. They should refer to all the criteria you've provided and follow your modeling.

9. Once you determine that students have practiced adequately, provide a quiet, isolated place for them to read aloud into a recorder. You might wish to designate one student to operate the recorder (trying to both read and operate the recorder could hinder a student's reading). Since tapes are inexpensive, you might supply one tape for each student. Be sure to label each tape with the title, author, and "professional reader's" name. Store each completed tape, along with its accompanying book, in a large lock-top plastic bag. Place these bags in your classroom Listening Center to be enjoyed by your students before the tapes go out to their intended audience. Let students enjoy the sound of their own voices!

SYSTEMATIC DECODING STRATEGIES

···○ **Explanation**

This lesson asks students to apply a familiar systematic decoding approach to upper-grade-level material. Thus, they are challenged to apply contextual reasoning and word analysis to the more complex texts they meet in these grades—including content area books and expository material.

···○ **Skill Focus**

Using decoding strategies for unknown or unfamiliar words; determining meaning of words and phrases using context clues; using the meanings of roots, prefixes and suffixes to determine the meaning of unknown words; applying self monitoring strategies

···○ **Materials & Resources**

Text

- Any grade-appropriate nonfiction or fiction text selection (Used in this lesson: Chief Joseph's surrender speech, which can be obtained from the PBS Web site: http://www.pbs.org/weta/thewest/ people/ a_c/chiefjoseph.htm)

Other

- 2 transparencies of partial section of selected text, one with targeted words completely masked out and the other with onsets of those words revealed

- Photocopies of complete selected text, with targeted words completely masked out

- Transparency or photocopies of complete text, with onsets of targeted words revealed

Note: This lesson provides a good opportunity to integrate reading strategies and content area study. See especially Step 2. The lesson can be taught effectively, however, with any appropriate text.

Prior to the Lesson: Go through the selected text and mask out words at different intervals. Choose words that are essential to the meaning of the sentence and that can be figured out fairly easily by use of context and/or onset (see masked-out words in Step 3 for examples).

STEPS

1. Tell students that today's lesson will review key decoding strategies. Good readers use strategies like this when they encounter unfamiliar words in a text they are reading.

2. (This step applies if you are using a content area selection; see Note, above.) If your students are already familiar with the informational background for the selection you've chosen, you'll merely need to review that background with them. If the text represents an area they have not yet studied, you can offer a brief overview to put it in context. For example, for the sample text, you might share something like the following:

   This speech was given during a period in United States history when the new settlers felt threatened by the Native Americans who had roamed free and lived in this land for many years. The U. S. Army decided to contain the Native Americans in a small section of land called a reservation. Imagine if our government told you that you could not leave your city to go anywhere. You would feel you had lost a lot of freedom, just as the Native Americans felt they had. A strong leader, Chief Joseph, decided to seek freedom for himself and his tribesmen in Canada. They traveled 1,100 miles but were attacked by the Army, which killed half of the 800 tribespeople. Just before reaching the Canadian border, Chief Joseph and his followers found themselves cornered by the Army. Chief Joseph had to make a difficult decision—continue and risk losing the lives of all his men, women, and children, or surrender and lose their freedom. He decided to surrender. It's at that point he wrote the famous speech we'll read today.

3. Now display the first transparency you've prepared. Think aloud as you read. Demonstrate how you make good guesses to supply the missing words. For this pass through, use only context. Write your best guesses above the masked-out words. An example based on the sample text follows:

Sample Text	Your Think-Aloud
I am tired of ▮▮▮▮. Our ▮▮▮▮ are killed.	"Well, I know that he and his tribe could be tired of running since they've traveled 1,100 miles already. Or maybe they're tired of fighting. I think *running* might be the best choice for now so I'll write that. The next blank is someone or something that has been killed. Could it be children, people, or men? I think I'll put *people* for now. That makes sense."

As a connection to your writing instruction, you might use the full text of Chief Joseph's speech to help students explore language and diction in greater depth. Challenge them to consider which words in the speech reflect the voice of a Native American Indian chief in the mid- to late-nineteenth century. Remind students that if they choose to write a first-person narrative from another person's point of view or to write dialogue that requires a particular voice or dialect, they must make wise word choices based on their audience and the circumstances. For example, Chief Joseph used "my children" rather than "my kids," as we might say today. He made reference to the earth, the sun, and the hills because Native Americans had a close relationship to the land. He also used simple language in his speech because English was not his first language.

4. Tell students that because you still have real doubts about the accuracy of your choices, you're going to use another kind of decoding clue. Display the second transparency, which reveals onsets (every letter before the first vowel) of each masked-out word and which provides a bit of additional context. Model how you use the sounds/letters and the new information to confirm or modify your original guesses. Demonstrate how you strike through incorrect guesses and write new ones. Call attention to the fact that the length of some words could also be clues. An example follows:

Sample Text	Your Think-Aloud
I am tired of f▇▇▇. Our ch▇ are killed. Looking Glass is dead. Toohoolhoolzote is dead.	"I chose *running*, but *fighting* was my other choice. Now I see that this word starts with an *f*, so I'll change my guess to *fighting*. The second word might be *children*, but that word looks shorter than *children*, which has eight letters. I wonder if it could be *chiefs* since I believe that Toohoolhoolzote and Looking Glass were chiefs. I'm going to put *chiefs*."

5. Tell students it's their turn. Set up partners. Distribute to each partner pair a photocopy of the complete text selection with masked-out words. Have students follow your model and write in their best guesses for the words.

6. Next distribute a photocopy (or display a transparency) of the second version of the complete text selection, with onsets revealed. Have students follow your model and use the new information to confirm or modify their guesses for the words.

7. Conclude by reading the entire selection aloud, pausing at the words that had been masked out so that students have a chance to check their work. Discuss with the class how a combination of context, onset, and word length can aid them in figuring out words in text. You might sum it up this way:

This process demonstrates a strategy for what you can do when you encounter a word in text that you don't know. First, you can ask yourself what makes sense. Second, you should give close attention to the way the word starts—every letter before the first vowel. Third, you should attend to the whole word—including its size. And you should use meaning throughout, always checking new informational clues to ask yourself if your guess makes sense.

Monitoring Comprehension

Gone are the days of assigning reading and expecting students to answer the questions at the end of the chapter. We've come to realize that assigning isn't teaching, that we must model reading strategies and give students adequate time to practice those strategies under our guidance. Yet, as mature readers, we are often not consciously aware of the thought processes we engage in while we are reading. Reading has become automatic. Therefore, one challenging aspect of teaching students to think about and monitor their comprehension during reading is refocusing our attention on the role of metacognition in our own reading. We need to quite purposefully think through how we ourselves think during reading so that we can verbalize and model this for students.

The research of Harris and Hodges (1995) defines metacognition as "knowing when what one is reading makes sense by monitoring and controlling one's own comprehension" (p. 39). Many students don't do this automatically. They need direct instruction to become aware of the intricacies of reading. To grasp the importance of metacognition instruction, consider the 2005 NAEP scores of both fourth and eighth graders in comprehension. They show that students performed markedly better on comprehension questions when they had experienced instruction in metacognitive skills such as drawing meaning from text by asking questions, summarizing the work, identifying key themes, and thinking critically about the author's purpose and whether that purpose was achieved (Wenglinsky, 2004).

Creating character dolls—as this sixth-grade class has done—is one way for readers to more deeply understand a story's characters.

The lessons in this section use a variety of approaches and techniques to help students develop into metacognitive, self-aware readers. For example, several of the lessons call students' attention to their "second voice." In *I Read It, but I Don't Get It!*, Cris Tovani (2000) notes that we have two voices that work in tandem during reading—one voice saying the words and one responding to the words. Because readers must activate both voices in order to be successfully, genuinely reading, we engage them here in recognizing the kinds of statements the second voice makes and then in creating simple symbols to codify the statements.

Other lessons help students track characters in a text, an especially important skill, as upper-grade texts increasingly involve numerous, complex characters. The strategies they learn now will even help them as they read convoluted novels as adults! In related lessons, students are asked to analyze and evaluate story elements. They probe characters' traits and motives, discern basic literary conflicts, and recognize and justify facts and opinions—all means of readers' developing awareness of and monitoring what they're reading. Another key lesson engages students and teachers in creating double-entry

After gathering clues about characters' traits in the novel *Holes*, this class used butcher paper and paint to design life-size characters.

journals, an invaluable way for readers to track their own reading and for teachers to gain insight into their students' thinking.

The entire section is geared toward helping students realize that reading is thinking. Upper-grade students need to be able to recognize that if they have stopped thinking, this is a problem and they need to have ready strategies to resolve the situation. Then, and only then, will they be in control of their ability to navigate text successfully.

TRACKING CHARACTERS

STEPS

1. Tell students that many adult readers (include yourself, if it applies!) have had a common experience when reading a novel: Several characters are introduced within just a few text pages and, when a character later reappears, readers aren't sure if they've ever met him or her before. Very soon, they're quite confused about who's who. Today you'll provide students with a way to avoid this dilemma—a way for them to remember characters and their traits as they go along.

2. Display the Characters I've Met transparency. Begin to read aloud a preselected story. As you encounter a character, stop and jot down the character's name on the transparency. If you already know—based on prior knowledge, the title, or the introduction—whether this is the main character or a minor character, check the appropriate box. Otherwise, wait to check off a box until the text clarifies the characters.

3. Continue reading aloud. As character traits are revealed, you'll do one of two things. If the trait is physical, you'll sketch a picture in the space provided and illustrate the trait. (If physical traits aren't explicitly described, you can nonetheless depict them by sketching how you imagine the character looks.) As nonphysical traits are presented, jot down those traits (and any related key words) on the lines provided.

4. Below is an example of how you might model your first steps in filling in the chart for the sample book:

What the Text Says	What the Teacher Says and Writes
Twilight was gathering, and Orpheus still wasn't here. Farid's heart beat faster, as it always did when day left him alone with the darkness.	"I need to jot down two characters, Orpheus and Farid. I don't know much about them yet." [Jot down characters' names.]
[T]he ghosts would soon begin to whisper. Farid knew only one place where he felt safe from them; right behind Dustfinger, so close that he could feel his warmth. Dustfinger wasn't afraid of the night. He liked it. (p. 1)	"There are two references to Farid's being afraid." [Write *fearful* on the lines in the column for Farid.]
	"Here's a third character, Dustfinger." [Write that name.] "What an odd name! Dustfinger seems to be brave—at least where the ghosts and night are mentioned." [Jot down *brave* and place *ghosts/night* in parentheses.]

5. Tell students it's their turn. Set up partners or small groups. Distribute to each pair or group a photocopy of the Characters I've Met chart. Have students use either assigned texts or independent narrative reading books and follow your model to fill in the chart for the characters in the story.

Explanation

Understanding characters in a narrative affects a reader's overall understanding of a piece. Students in the upper grades are fully capable of identifying characters in narratives. Because of the increasing sophistication of the text, however, they need strategies to help them sort out the who's who of the text and to analyze the development of each character. This lesson will help them do just that!

Skill Focus

Monitoring comprehension; identifying characters; analyzing characters' traits and motives; paraphrasing and summarizing using main ideas, events, details, and themes; using a graphic organizer

Materials & Resources

Text

- A narrative text with a main and several minor characters (Used in this lesson: *Inkspell* by Cornelia Funke)

Other

- Transparency of Characters I've Met form (Appendix, p. 118)

- Photocopies, 1 for each pair or group, of same form

Bonus Ideas

After reading a text selection, have students list the names of characters they've met. Write each name on a separate index card. Count the number of cards and ask for that many volunteers to come forward. Have each volunteer choose a card. Students are to introduce the character on their card to the class as if they were at a party, introducing two people who had never met before.

CLUES TO A CHARACTER'S CHARACTER

Explanation

Students need to be taught explicitly to study all possible clues about characters so that they can grasp each as deeply as possible. This lesson builds on the previous lesson by showing students three key sources for information about a story's characters. Students culminate their inquiry by pulling all the information together in a descriptive summary.

Skill Focus

Identifying characters; analyzing characters' traits and motives; paraphrasing and summarizing using main ideas and details; using a graphic organizer

Materials & Resources

Text

- A narrative text with a clear main character and several other characters (Used in this lesson: *The Yellow Star: The Legend of King Christian X of Denmark* by Carmen Agra Deedy)

Other

- Multiple copies of the same text for students
- Transparency of Character Clues (Appendix, p. 119)
- Photocopies, 1 for each partner set, of this appendix

Bonus Ideas

Assemble newspaper pictures and captions that illustrate human behavior and/or traits: a soldier helping a child; an arson-related fire; and so on. Glue the pictures onto a large paper banner. Under the pictures, students should write adjectives that describe relevant character traits.

STEPS

1. Remind students that the more fully readers grasp the different angles and complexities of a story's characters, the better they will truly comprehend everything else about the story. Tell students that there are three ways that writers typically develop their characters. In today's lesson you'll look for these three ways—what a character does, what he or she says, and what others say about him or her—and sort out the clues.

2. Display the transparency and point out the three columns to students. Display as well your selected text. Tell students that you will be looking for clues that fall into these three categories. You will start with the main character. (See chart below.)

3. Starting with the cover, read aloud until you encounter information that identifies the main character. For example, for the sample text, you would immediately note that the main character is likely King Christian X because the book's title reveals this. Write that name in the appropriate row. Continue reading. As you come to them, note trait-revealing clues and write them in the appropriate columns. An example follows:

What Character Says:	What Character Does:	What Speaker and/or Others Say:
". . . be prepared to shoot the king—for I will be that soldier."	He has the Nazi flag removed.	". . . the Danes held one thing in common: all were loyal subjects of their beloved King Christian."
"Of course! You would hide it among its sisters."	He worries about his people.	
"And, do you understand what this means?"	He wears the Star of David to set an example for his people.	". . . a king so loved needs no bodyguard."

Summary   From all three sources, I think that King Christian was a man of high integrity and a strong, ingenious leader who protected his subjects from great harm.

4. Conclude your modeling by demonstrating how you use the clues you've gathered to create a summary description of the character. An example for the sample text follows is shown above.

5. Tell students it's their turn. Set up partners. Distribute to each partner pair a photocopy of the Character Clues chart and a copy of the selected text. Have students follow your model and fill in the chart for several minor characters in the story. Invite partners to compare their conclusions about the characters.

LIFE-SIZE CHARACTERS

Explanation

This lesson works well as a follow-up to the two previous lessons about character analysis. Through fun group work in writing and art, it challenges students to delve even further into examining all aspects of a character. It also offers a great way to engage students who exhibit different learning styles and strengths.

Skill Focus

Analyzing character traits and motives; rereading to find details; responding to texts through writing and graphic arts; using a graphic organizer; creating mental images; skimming and scanning; paraphrasing and summarizing using main ideas and details; classifying and categorizing ideas

Materials & Resources

Text

- Multiple copies of a grade-appropriate narrative text with a clearly described main character

Other

- Photocopies, 1 for each team, of Character Analysis chart (Appendix, p. 120)

- Large sheet of white butcher paper

- Several sheets of lined paper

- Markers, crayons, or paint

Bonus Ideas

Supplement this lesson by having students complete a biographical sketch based on their researched notes. Then, one student might stand (literally, using the butcher paper outline) in the shoes of the character and read aloud the sketch.

STEPS

1. Review with students what they have learned about character analysis in the previous two lessons. Remind them that overall comprehension is greatly affected by a reader's understanding of the characters in a story. Explain that today the class will break into teams to complete an intensive analysis of a story's main character. Each team will look at the character from a different angle.

2. Organize the class into four groups. Because each group will be working on a different aspect of character analysis, you may want to set up the groups based on students' preferences and strengths. Distribute a copy of the same story to each group. As a class, identify the main character.

3. Have all groups read the story.

4. Next, hand out photocopies of the Character Analysis chart to each team. In addition, distribute a sheet of lined paper to the first three groups and a blank sheet of butcher paper to the fourth. Instruct the teams to fill in the organizer. Each team is to use different criteria, as described below:

   Group 1: Personality Team—Research character's personality by examining traits (such as shyness, kindness, rudeness) and feelings (such as loneliness, anxiety, happiness).

   Group 2: Motive Team—Research character's reasons for actions and behavior, such as revenge, survival, and making friends.

   Group 3: Action Team—Research character's actions, such as what the character specifically does to solve problems.

   Group 4: Art Team—Research character's appearance, such as the look of the character's face, physical demeanor, and clothing.

5. After students have completed the charts, have the first three groups use the information to each write a summary paragraph targeted to their assignment. Have the fourth group make a life-size outline by tracing a group member lying down on the butcher paper. They should then add appropriate elements to create the look they have researched.

6. Conclude by bringing teams back together to share their findings. Discuss how all the information they have gathered combines to provide a full character analysis. You might want to make a culminating hallway display by placing the life-size character outline at the center and attaching the summaries around or within the outline.

TWO VOICES OF A GOOD READER

Scholastic Teaching Resources

Explanation

This lesson helps make students aware of the two clear voices that good readers rely upon. One voice reads the words and the other constantly responds to what is read. In order for a reader to achieve genuine comprehension, both voices need to be "heard" loud and clear. That's done here by explicitly illustrating how a reader's inner voice comments on what is being read.

Skill Focus

Monitoring comprehension; using prior knowledge; making connections between text and personal experience or world events; making text-to-text connections

Materials & Resources

Text
- Any grade-appropriate fiction or nonfiction text

Other
- Colored chalk

Bonus Ideas

You might occasionally have students read as partners. Assign each partner the role of one of the voices of a reader: The first voice/student reads the text orally, the other responds aloud. They can trade roles every page.

STEPS

1. Using different-colored chalk for each, draw two large profiles facing each other. (See diagram at the end of the lesson.) Tell students that today they're going to learn about the two voices that all good readers have.

2. Explain that you'll model the two voices to let the class know how these voices sound. Read aloud from your preselected text. Pause after reading one or two paragraphs and say something like, "One voice of a reader is what you just heard. This voice says the words, sometimes out loud but usually silently. Even when readers are reading silently, they are pronouncing the words and hearing them inside their heads."

3. Now draw a speech bubble coming from the mouth of the profile on the left. Copy into that bubble a few words or a sentence from the text you have just read.

4. Explain that a reader's second voice performs a different job: It responds to what is being read. Although both voices are usually silent, they are constantly interacting.

5. Read aloud another paragraph and remind students that what they've just heard is the first voice again. Then stop and respond to the text you've read. You might make comments like:

   "This is . . .

   - . . . interesting."
   - . . . new to me."
   - . . . something I already knew. "
   - . . . important. "
   - . . . like something I've experienced. "
   - . . . similar to something I've read about. "
   - . . . like something I've heard on the news."

6. In the profile on the right—in the area of the brain—write in several of the comments you've just made. Stress again the importance of both voices of a reader. Both the one that reads the words and the one that responds to what has been read are critical to comprehension.

CODING TEXT

Explanation

In the previous lesson, students learned about the two voices of a good reader. Now they are ready to learn a special way of coding a reader's second voice—the one that expresses thoughts and reflections. Coding text causes students to slow down in their reading and examine their cognitive processes. You won't want to have students do this too often as it does reduce their reading rate, but it's valuable as a means of demonstrating the complexities of reading. And it's fun, too—students love "secret" codes!

Skill Focus

Monitoring comprehension; using prior knowledge; making connections between text and personal experience or world events; making text-to-text connections; responding to texts through a variety of methods and through different perspectives; creating mental images to aid comprehension

Materials & Resources

Text

- Any grade-appropriate informational text (Used in this lesson: an article based on a children's newspaper feature, "World of Wonder: Snowflakes," Triefeldt Studios, in *The State*)

Other

- Transparency of the text selection

- For each student: 1 or 2 VIP strips (each snipped 4 times to form 5 fingers)

STEPS

1. Review the previous lesson with students. Have them describe the two voices of a reader. Tell students that in this lesson they'll work more with the second voice.

2. For this second voice, ask the class to help you brainstorm the types of things that readers think about as they read. List them on the board.

3. As you list the items, ask students to help you come up with a symbol for each. A sample list, with possible symbols, is at right.

4. Display the transparency. Read the text aloud and model how you use your second voice to respond to what you're reading. For each reflection, write in the appropriate symbol. Include

Reflections and Symbols	
This is interesting.	☺
This is dull.	✗
This is something I already know.	✓
This is new to me.	★
I want to be sure to remember this.	+
That's cool!	!
What does that mean?	?
I want to know more about that.	△
I can picture that.	◉ ◉

a variety of the reflections and symbols your class has generated. An example coded version of the sample text is below:

Shape Shifting

A snowflake begins as a tiny supercooled water droplet (✓) that meets a speck of dust called ice nuclei, (!) or freezing nuclei. The water vapor begins to evaporate on the surface of the ice nuclei and develops facets—changing into a hexagonal prism. (!) As the crystal falls, it grows larger and arms may begin to sprout. (◉ ◉) This is called branching. (+) The final shape of a snow crystal . . .

5. Have students get out their assigned texts or independent reading books. Distribute VIP strips to each student. Instruct them to follow your model as they read. They should pay special attention to their second voice, pausing when they note a specific reaction. At that point in the text, they should place a "finger" and write on it the appropriate symbol to code their reflections and reactions.

RECORDING REFLECTIONS: DOUBLE-ENTRY JOURNAL

Explanation

The double-entry journal is a unique means of getting students to slow down in their reading and process text in a teacher-guided way. This method comes as close as any to looking inside the reader's mind to find out how he or she interprets text. Extremely versatile, it can be used across disciplines. In this lesson, you model the use of the technique and then provide an opportunity for students to try it out.

Skill Focus

Monitoring comprehension; using prior knowledge; making connections between text and personal experience or world events; responding to texts through different perspectives and methods

Materials & Resources

Text

- A fiction or nonfiction text with passages that require careful thought and interpretation (Used in this lesson: *And Still the Turtle Watched* by Sheila MacGill-Callahan)

Other

- Transparency of Double-Entry Journal Sample Page (Appendix, p. 120), prepared as described in Prior to the Lesson

- For each student: photocopy of the same form, prepared as described in Prior to the Lesson

Bonus Ideas

Challenge students to keep their own Double-Entry Journals by writing down interesting excerpts as they read and then responding to those excerpts in a separate column.

Prior to the Lesson: *Determine points in the sample text that you feel need a reader's extra thought and interpretation. Jot down excerpts from those passages, along with their page numbers, on the left side of the Double-Entry Journal Sample Page (Appendix, p. 120). Allow sufficient space among passages so that a reader could add his or her own written responses on the right side of the journal page. (See example in Step 3.) Follow the same procedure for creating a model Double-Entry Journal page for students, but with different text excerpts from those you used for the transparency.*

STEPS

1. Tell students that today they'll learn another way to pay attention to the second voice of a reader. In this technique, they'll have a chance to record their reflections and thoughts about text in a special journal. The fact that each response is uniquely a reader's own means that it cannot be incorrect (this is usually quite an appealing aspect and may free up some students to respond openly).

2. Display the transparency of the Double-Entry Journal Sample Page with the left side already filled in (see Prior to the Lesson). Discuss the format with the class.

3. Begin to read aloud the sample text. Stop at the first page noted in the left column and reread that text section particularly carefully. Think aloud about what the author might be saying here. For the first notation, you might say, "I think this is an interesting way for the author to show how time is passing. She has used colors to describe the passing seasons and has done it with few words. Let me write that on the right side of this journal." Add those comments on the right side of the model journal page. An example, showing two notations, is at right.

The text says . . .	I think . . .
p. 6: He watched the green . . . He watched the gold . . . He watched the white . . .	The author is showing time passing by using colors to represent the seasons. Pretty clever!
p. 8: "The Great Bear chased the Little Bear around the Northern sky."	The Great and Little Bears are constellations in the sky. If they are revolving, it means again that time is passing—maybe even years!

4. Now distribute to each student a photocopy of a Double-Entry Journal page on which you have written several short excerpts from the same text. Let students experiment with responding as they read.

The Strategic Reader

Explanation

Students will find that rereading is a helpful strategy in many different situations—for example, they can use it to fix comprehension when they've lost track of what they're reading or to gain a new understanding of the information. This lesson provides an opportunity for students to experience firsthand how reading something through once is not necessarily enough. There's an additional component built into this lesson as well, as students find out how different it is to read with and without a purpose.

Skill Focus

Using rereading to find details and to self-correct; responding to text through a variety of methods, such as drama, writing, and art; using graphic organizers; skimming and scanning for information

Materials & Resources

Text

- Any grade-appropriate fiction or nonfiction reading selection that lends itself to critical thinking-level questions; or a grade-level sample state reading assessment

Other

- Photocopies, 1 for each student, of the sample text

- Set of questions, either prepared by teacher or provided with sample test

- Different-colored sticky notes, 1 of each color for each student

- 2 pieces of chart paper

- Marker

Prior to the Lesson: *If you are not using a prepared test, create a set of questions based on your sample text. The questions should involve critical thinking so that readers are challenged beyond the literal level.*

Steps

1. Tell students that today's lesson will start with a reading activity. Distribute two different-colored sticky notes to each student along with the preselected reading passage. Instruct students to read the first two or three paragraphs only once and then to immediately turn the passage over so that they can no longer see the text. For this reading, do not provide a purpose or guiding question.

2. When all students have finished, ask a question about the text. Have students write an answer, asking everyone to use the same-colored sticky note. Students who feel they don't know the answer should simply write, "I don't know." (Students should not put their names on the notes.) Collect the sticky notes.

3. At this point, engage students in a brief class discussion about what readers can do if they're stumped for an answer to a question or if they simply feel they haven't understood what they've read. Guide the discussion to focus on rereading as a repair or fix-it strategy.

4. Now read the same question aloud. Have students turn their papers over and reread the first paragraph. Immediately upon finishing their reading, students are to write a response to the question on the remaining sticky note. Tell students that if they feel their first answer was correct, they should rewrite that response and put a checkmark next to it to show that they have reread carefully and confirmed their original thinking. Tell students, too, that if they have decided to change their first responses, that is also fine. Collect the sticky notes, which should all be the same color, as each student finishes.

5. Mount the two pieces of chart paper. Title one "Correct Response" and the other "Incorrect Response." Reveal and discuss the correct answer with the class and write it on the chart paper directly below the appropriate title.

6. Next, read aloud each sticky note from the first reading. With students' input, decide whether it is a correct or an incorrect response and attach it to the appropriate chart. Total up the sticky notes on each chart. The "Incorrect Response" chart will likely contain more notes than the other chart. Assure students that this is okay. Remind them that they hadn't done any rereading for this set of responses.

Bonus Ideas

Using recipes, following directions, or reading a how-to are some other ways to teach rereading. For example, discuss with students what might happen if a chef did not reread to check whether a recipe called for a tablespoon (T) or teaspoon (t) of sugar. Too much or too little of this ingredient would result in a creation that was either overly sweet or bitter. The same is true for following map directions or reading how-to assembly directions. Not rereading might result in a toy or a piece of furniture that winds up looking very odd, indeed!

7. Follow the same procedure for the second set of sticky notes. Each chart will now contain a myriad of notes, color-coded for each reading. The completed "Correct Response" chart will likely contain more notes that reflect the second reading.

8. Engage the class in a discussion about the charts. Why and how did the second reading result in a greater number of correct answers? List students' ideas on the board. Try to include at least the following two important reasons:

   Students had the opportunity to reread the text, so they could search for and locate details to answer the question.

   Students had a purpose for listening the second time; they knew the question.

9. Using the additional questions—either as a whole class or with students working independently—repeat this same process throughout the entire sample text.

FACT AND OPINION

Explanation

Differentiating between fact and opinion often confuses students. The skill is an important part of their becoming discriminating readers—readers who know they must continually analyze and evaluate text. In this lesson, students are invited to work with real-life reading materials—newspaper articles—as they sort fact from opinion.

Skill Focus

Differentiating between fact and opinion; skimming and scanning; using graphic organizers; rereading to find details and to self-correct; coding text

Materials & Resources

Text

- For student work: A newspaper article that includes at least 6–8 facts and the same number of opinions, and that utilizes key opinion words and phrases (see Step 3)

- For modeling: An alternate newspaper article that includes fact and opinion statements

Other

- Photocopies, 1 for each small group, of the newspaper article

- For each small group: 2 different-colored highlighters, a sheet of unlined paper, several pairs of scissors, and glue sticks

Bonus Ideas

- To reinforce the difference between fact and opinion, read *Flying Solo* by Ralph Fletcher. One character, Christopher, always says "fact" or "opinion" after another character speaks.

Prior to the Lesson: Comb through the alternate newspaper article to locate two statements of fact and two statements of opinion. Try to find opinion statements that include the key words or phrases listed in Step 3. Write the statements on separate sentence strips.

STEPS

1. In any order, display the four model sentence strips you've prepared. Ask for volunteers to help you identify and sort the four statements into two sets—one set of fact statements and one set of opinion statements. Call on other students to help you define the difference between the two kinds of statements. Elicit definitions such as "A fact is something that can be proven to be true" and "An opinion is a personal view that is neither right nor wrong and that can be disputed."

2. Invite students to share additional facts and opinions. Hold a brief class discussion to analyze each statement and to evaluate whether it has been correctly identified.

3. Now tell students that certain key words or phrases are often used in opinion statements. These words can provide clues to distinguishing opinions from facts. With help from the class, brainstorm and write on the board a list of such words and phrases. One possible list follows:

perhaps	I believe	best	maybe
in my opinion	I like	worst	probably
I think	I feel	should	most

4. Set up several small groups. Distribute to each group a photocopy of the selected newspaper article, a sheet of paper, two highlighters, scissors, and glue sticks. Have students read the article carefully, thinking about facts and opinions as they read.

5. Now instruct students to locate and highlight opinions in the article. Remind them to refer to the brainstormed list but be sure they realize that not all opinion statements will include one of these words or phrases.

6. Next have students skim through the article to locate facts and to use the different-colored marker to highlight them.

7. Instruct each group to use the sheet of paper to draw a T-chart. They are to title one side of the T-chart "Facts" and the other side "Opinions."

8. Finally, have students cut out all the highlighted statements and paste them on the appropriate side of the T-chart. Invite groups to discuss their decisions and charts with one another.

ANALYZING CONFLICTS

Explanation

In the lower grades, readers learn that all narratives have problems and solutions. By the upper grades, narrative text becomes more sophisticated, and upper-grade readers need to be able not only to identify a problem but also to categorize it according to the five basic literary conflicts. This lesson introduces students to the categories and challenges them to analyze a text and figure out its basic conflict, and then to use this knowledge to search for and identify the basic conflicts in newspaper articles.

Skill Focus

Analyzing the basic types of conflicts; monitoring comprehension

Materials & Resources

Text

- A short story or narrative book with a sophisticated theme appropriate for upper grades (Used in this lesson: *More Than Anything Else* by Marie Bradby)

- 5–10 preselected newspapers

Other

- Blank transparency

Bonus Ideas

Write the names of five common folk and fairy tales on index cards (one story per card). Set up small groups and give one card to each group. Invite group members to discuss the story and decide which conflict it represents. Take a few minutes to have each group describe the story and conflict to the whole class. Invite class discussion and offer any necessary clarification.

STEPS

1. Review with students that nearly all narrative text is structured around a problem and its resolution. Explain that today students will learn that this problem almost always stems from a set of basic conflicts. There are five basic conflicts, each of which involves a person or persons—the main character and perhaps other characters. In each basic conflict, an individual or individuals struggle with one of five different antagonists or enemies.

2. On the board or a transparency, list the five basic conflicts and briefly discuss each. Below is an example list:

    Self: Individual struggles with his or her own conscience or body in some way.

    Human: Individual struggles with another person.

    Society: Individual struggles with what the greater world expects of him or her.

    Machine: Individual struggles with a machine—something industrial or technological.

    Nature: Individual struggles with the natural elements—cold, snow, heat, water, fire, and so on.

3. Display the preselected story or short novel. Alert students to listen carefully as you read it and to keep in mind the list of basic conflicts. Read aloud a short story. Ask students to help you identify the type of conflict experienced by the main character, and engage the class in a discussion about how the author has made this conflict the center of the story. For example, the sample book, which is biographical but structured like a narrative short story, describes a terrible dilemma facing a famous African American (Booker T. Washington). More than anything, this young man wants to learn to read but is told that people of his skin color at this point in history cannot be educated to read. In the end, he is able to fulfill his thirst for literacy and is taught to read and write by another African American. (In this story, the basic conflict is individual vs. society. Some students might choose individual vs. another person, and that position, if defended well, might also be valid.)

4. Organize the class into five small groups and distribute a preselected newspaper to each group. Have students search for articles that reflect each of the five basic conflict categories. Instruct them to write, or to be ready to discuss, the reasoning behind their decisions.

5. Bring the class together to share their findings.

WHAT'S IT ALL ABOUT?

Explanation

This lesson offers a novel way to get your content reading as well as your literature instruction off and running. Besides allowing some brief movement in the classroom, which is still necessary in the upper grades, it taps students' deductive reasoning ability and helps ultimately to guide them through text. As part of a "detective mission" to discover the overall topic of a text, they are forced to stop and intentionally process interesting new information.

Skill Focus

Monitoring comprehension; finding details; self-correcting; asking questions to aid comprehension; making predictions; drawing conclusions/making inferences; making connections

Materials & Resources

Text

• Multiple copies of a grade-appropriate fiction or nonfiction text (Used in this lesson: "The World's Wildest Horse Race" from *The Wild Side: Extreme Sports* by McGraw-Hill/Jamestown Education)

Other

• 1 phrase strip for each student (see Prior to the Lesson)

Bonus Ideas

This lesson is a quick and easy way to engage students in content area lessons as well. You might even let different groups of students read ahead, gather the interesting facts, and prepare the strips for the lesson. They'll enjoy challenging their classmates!

Prior to the Lesson: Read through the preselected text to locate about a dozen interesting phrases that hint at but don't completely divulge the main idea. List these phrases on a sheet of paper, spacing them widely. Make photocopies and cut the phrases apart. (Make enough copies so that each student can receive a phrase.) Possible phrases for the sample book are at right.

the Goose, Wolf, Ram, Snail
pots of dirt rushed to her
body wrapped in the flag of the contrada
horse is taken to the church
each contrada hires guard
young men dressed in wigs and medieval clothes
two sharp turns and lies on the pitch of a hillside
around the course three times to win
wear steel helmets for protection
slam each other into walls covered with mattresses
faint from the excitement

STEPS

1. Explain to students that good readers stop at intervals during reading—especially as they encounter interesting new information—to think about and process what they're reading.

2. Tell students that in this lesson they'll have a chance to act as "detectives on a mission." That mission is to use clues to try to figure out the overall topic of a text. The clues are phrases of interesting information from the text.

3. Arrange students in small groups. Distribute one phrase strip to each student. Instruct students to read and memorize their phrase quickly.

4. Set a timer. Tell students they have one minute to get up and approach as many classmates as possible to give their clue and to listen to what their classmates have to share. After one minute, ask students to return to their small groups. Each group now has four minutes to study their assembled clues and to use them to guess the overall topic of the text.

5. Call on each group to share what they've identified as a topic. As groups will each have gathered a body of different clues, it's a good idea to allow for some debate. After each group has shared, give everyone another clue. Reveal either the title or a text illustration. (For the sample text, an illustration might be the best since it won't give away as much as the title.) Now have each group state whether they'd like to revise or stay with their original hypothesis and to briefly explain why.

6. Distribute copies of the story to students. Explain that the phrases are all in the text. They are to stop during reading when they encounter a familiar clue (phrase). They should consider each carefully in terms of their prediction about the overall topic.

7. Finally, have all students work together to piece together the correct overall topic or main idea of the piece. (For the sample book, the topic is a wild and crazy horse race in Italy that is accompanied by much tradition!)

Generating and Answering Questions

Voltaire, the great French writer and thinker, once said, "Judge others by their questions rather than by their answers." Surely, asking good, thought-provoking questions is the mark of an inquisitive mind. Searching for the answers—even when that search does not end successfully—is a noble and ambitious goal for us all. As perhaps the ultimate example, Albert Einstein claimed to have had no special powers other than, as he put it, being "passionately curious"—having questions that inspired his thinking and his acquisition of great knowledge.

While we do, of course, recognize the importance of our students' doing well in testing situations, how often those of us in education feel it would be a blessing to concentrate more on questions rather than correct answers! Questions, especially those that are generated by natural curiosity, are the best motivators and catalysts we have in education, if not in our lives. Not surprisingly, our questions and desire for answers also drive us as readers.

From the moment good readers hold a book in their hands, they start to wonder about it and to formulate questions. They ask themselves:

- What kind of book do I think this is?

- Have I read other books by this author?

- What were they about?

- Do I know anything about this topic?

Generating questions and predictions and then reading to confirm or modify the predictions helps focus a student's reading.

And that's just the beginning—the pre-reading part. During reading, good readers are continually generating questions about the meaning of the text. In a fictional piece, they are wondering what a character will do next or how one plot twist will connect to another. In a nonfiction piece, they are assimilating facts that lead to unanticipated discoveries and further questions about those discoveries. It's an unending process, during which some questions are answered as others are formulated. And, after the reading is done, unanswered questions often remain. This simply means good readers have further inquiry, reading, and research ahead. In fact, a recurring series of questions and answers is what good reading is all about.

It follows, therefore, that instruction that focuses on questioning will improve students' reading. As the National Reading Panel reports: There is "strong empirical and scientific evidence that instruction of question generation during reading benefits reading comprehension in terms of memory and answering questions based on text as well as integrating and identifying main ideas through summarization" (NRPR; NICHHD, 2000, p. 4-88).

This section covers questioning from many different angles. Two lessons focus on the importance of readers' making predictions and generating their own questions both before and during reading. Several other lessons engage students in posing essential guiding questions that need to be asked as readers approach a text: Is this a book I would really like to read? What was the author's purpose in writing this text? From what point of view is this text written and how do I know that? These are key questions readers should pose throughout their lives, and students in these upper grades need to feel comfortable formulating and considering them in their daily reading.

Because so much reading is done electronically these days, several lessons explore reading on the Internet—a quite different phenomenon from reading regular text. One pair of Internet-based lessons walks students through the process of using search engines effectively for research. A second set of lessons tackles Internet credibility. How does a reader/consumer recognize propaganda on the Internet? How can we help students evaluate the validity and quality of Internet materials?

A good teacher can take the enthusiasm and natural curiosity of young learners and turn it to the child's great benefit in reading. It doesn't always make for a quiet, predictable classroom, but after all, we don't want our students to be quiet, passive learners: Encouraging the "noise" and the questions is part of the good teacher's job. Let's use their inquisitive nature as the catalyst for their becoming good readers! The lessons in this section should help you do just that. Have fun!

GENERATING QUESTIONS BEFORE AND DURING READING

Explanation

Good reading is not a matter of answering teacher-generated questions about a text. Instead, students need to realize that good readers are constantly asking and answering their own questions. In this lesson, students will enjoy creating little "finger" flap booklets and then recording and answering questions as they read.

Skill Focus

Generating and answering questions; establishing a purpose for reading; skimming and scanning for information

Materials & Resources

Text

- A grade-appropriate informational text (Used in this lesson: *Animal Sharpshooters* by Anthony Fredericks)

Other

- 1 sheet of unlined paper for teacher and for each student
- Pair of scissors for each student

Bonus Ideas

On the classroom wall, mount a large piece of butcher paper to form a graffiti wall. Title it "Questions We Have." Instruct students to use a marker to add questions—from this lesson and/or from ongoing reading—and encourage them to do research as time permits. The answers can be written underneath the questions on the wall so that everyone can be better informed.

STEPS

1. Tell students that in this lesson they will learn how to pose and answer questions about factual text. In this way, they will be able to tap into their own natural curiosity to discover key information.

2. Hold up your sheet of paper and fold it in half lengthwise. Unfold it and make four to five horizontal cuts from the right edge to the fold. This will create a little booklet, with the snipped "fingers" forming the front cover. (See diagram below.)

3. Display the preselected text and call attention to the cover. Say something like, "All good readers look at the cover and title of what they're reading and immediately have questions. For example, this book's title is *Animal Sharpshooters*. The cover picture shows some sort of lizard with a very long tongue. It's reaching out to a grasshopper. I'm wondering whether this animal is defending itself or getting a meal. I hope I'll find out as I read."

4. Show students the little booklet again. On the top finger, write the question: "Is this lizard defending or eating?" Continue to read the text aloud. Stop at the end of each page or section and model how you form a question about something you've read. Write the questions on the remaining booklet fingers.

5. As you read, stop as well when you encounter an answer to one of the questions you've posed. Open the appropriate flap and jot down the answer on the space underneath.

Is this lizard defending or eating?
Blood is squirting from its eyes.
How does the spider throw its web?
How far can the skipper butterfly shoot a pellet?
Does the sea cucumber's stomach detach itself?

6. Caution students that answers aren't always found in the text. If this occurs during your modeling, tell students that this is one strong motivation for people to do research—searching further for the answers to otherwise unanswered questions.

7. Distribute copies of the text, an unlined sheet of paper, and a pair of scissors to each student. Have students follow your model to create booklets. Then have them generate a different question from the one you modeled for either the title or the cover. Instruct them to then pick up from where you left off in your reading, pausing just as you did to generate and record questions and answers. Unanswered questions can be posed for whole-class discussion and/or recorded on a graffiti wall (see Bonus Ideas).

TWO-PART LESSON: ELECTRONIC Q AND A

PART 1: STREAMLINING TO FIND ESSENTIAL KEY WORDS

···O Explanation

The Internet has made reference materials highly accessible and has greatly simplified the task of doing research. Although most young students are more familiar with the Internet than are many teachers, they still need help streamlining their searches. This two-part lesson offers students a means of doing just that. In this first part, students learn how to streamline their research questions and pinpoint key words. Learning to do this kind of focused pruning also helps develop students' reading skills such as locating information by using a book's table of contents, index, headings, and key terms.

···O Skill Focus

Generating and answering questions; classifying and categorizing; establishing a purpose for reading; skimming and scanning for information

···O Materials & Resources

Text
- For modeling: 1 search question
- For student work: list of search questions

Other
- Transparency or sentence strips of search questions
- 1 sheet of unlined paper for each partner set or small group

Prior to the Lesson: Prepare a list of research questions that lend themselves to the kind of pruning illustrated in this lesson (i.e., using the fewest key words possible to search most effectively). Write each question on a separate sentence strip or make a transparency of your complete list. (See Step 7.)

STEPS

1. You might want to start this two-part lesson by sharing how research was conducted in the "old days." It typically involved all-day excursions to the library where long hours were spent among the stacks consulting encyclopedias and searching for reference books. (The point here is not to paint libraries in a negative light but to help students gain appreciation for the easy access they now have to many reference sources, an ease many simply take for granted.)

2. Explain that the challenges researchers face today are quite different. One challenge is evaluating the authenticity of the sources they find because not every Internet site is legitimate. (See pages 49–51 for an evaluation activity.) The challenge you'll focus on today is how to home in on the material you're really looking for. Almost everything is available at one's fingertips! So researchers need to streamline their search to avoid wasting hours of weeding through unrelated information. Explain that the best choice of key words will typically allow a researcher to reach the desired information efficiently and quickly.

3. Tell students that today's lesson focuses on choosing the truly essential key words that will enable them to find answers to research questions via an Internet search engine. In tomorrow's lesson they'll actually get to use a computer to try out their words.

4. Demonstrate, step by step, how you streamline your own search in order to find the answer to a question. On the board write a question like this:

   What was the most deadly volcanic eruption ever recorded in history?

5. Point out that this sentence has 11 words. Tell students you know that that is far more than you'll need for your search, and that typing in the unnecessary words will bring far too many, inexact results. Think aloud as you walk them through an analysis of why you should retain or discard each word. An example, based on the sample question, follows:

   - *What:* Almost all questions have a *who, what, when, where,* or *how* word. I'm thinking that word is too general to be a key word for a search engine. It might be a more important word on a test. But that's different from using a search engine.

Bonus Ideas

You might bookmark Education World's Hunt the Fact Monster section at http://www.education world.com/a_lesson/factmonster for student research. It offers weekly questions and answers that students can use to go on computer-based "scavenger hunts." Not only will students have fun going on these searches, but they'll get great experience in locating correct answers to questions at the same time!

- *Was:* Verbs are rarely used in Internet searches. Sometimes descriptive adjectives and adverbs might be necessary to narrow the search, but I'm usually searching for a person, place, event, or thing—all nouns. I won't use this word.

- *The:* Articles like *a*, *an*, and *the* would never be used in a search engine.

- *Most:* I won't use this word for the search because it's such a general word. I think I can find the most deadly eruption after I get to a specific site.

- *Deadly:* I think this one might be an important word in my search because if I search simply for volcanic eruptions without including deadly, I'll get all kinds of information about volcanoes. I'll find information about what causes them to erupt, what happens when they erupt, and other things that might be interesting but will not give me what I'm looking for. So, I'll use this word.

- *Volcanic:* Yes, I'll definitely use this word. I think the type of eruption is very important.

- *Eruption:* I think this might be the most important word to use. It is the noun that states what my basic search is about.

- *Ever:* I think this word isn't necessary. If I find deadly volcanic eruption, I'm sure I'll find the most deadly ever.

- *Recorded:* It's obvious that if there had been a more deadly volcanic eruption that wasn't recorded, then I'm not going to find it because no one recorded it! So I think this just restates the obvious and I won't use it.

- *In:* I don't think I'll ever need a preposition in my search.

- *History:* Again, I don't think this word is necessary. It just gives more background for things that are recorded.

- **My Conclusion:** So, I've narrowed this long sentence down to three words. Here are the three words that I'll use for my search: *deadly volcanic eruption*.

6. Organize the class into partners or small groups. Either distribute one sentence strip to each partner or group, or display a transparency of a list of research questions and have students select a question and write it down.

7. Have students follow your model to prune down their sentence to the fewest key words that will allow them to find the answer most quickly. (Remind them that this means having to navigate the fewest links and the fewest scroll-downs.) Have them write their pared-down key words on a sheet of paper. Below is a list of possible questions:

   - In what location did Jane Goodall spend most of her life studying wild chimpanzees?

   - How long does a baby koala stay protected in its mother's pouch?

   - What is the longest distance ever traveled by a hot air balloon?

   - In what year was the first typewriter invented?

   - What is in the screen of an LCD television?

   - Who holds the record for the fastest marathon?

   - What is the population of the largest country in South America?

8. Tell students that they are now ready to try out their key-word choices and will do so in Part 2 of this lesson. Be sure they keep today's work handy.

TWO-PART LESSON: ELECTRONIC Q AND A

PART 2: SEARCHING AND SKIMMING

Explanation

In this Part 2 lesson, students get to put their streamlined search questions to the test as they actually input their questions. Including a point system for scoring adds a game-like competitive element to the lesson. Ahead of time, you'll want to find a safe search engine with established parameters within which your students can work comfortably.

Skill Focus

Generating and answering questions; classifying and categorizing; establishing a purpose for reading; skimming and scanning for information

Materials & Resources

Text

- Students' pared-down questions from Part 1 of this lesson

Other

- Internet access for teachers and students

- Identified, approved search engines (Used in this lesson for teacher modeling: Google.com; for students' possibilities, see Bonus Ideas)

Bonus Ideas

You might check out these kid-friendly search engines: ask.com (formerly Ask Jeeves for Kids; no site on the Cyberpatrol block list is used); KidsClick! (backed by many librarians); Looksmart's Kids Directory (sites handpicked by employees of the company); Yahooligans (the most established childrens' directory).

STEPS

1. Tell students that today they will get to try their chosen key words to locate answers to their questions. Explain that the class will be playing a kind of game as they search. The partner or group to accumulate the fewest number of points will be the winner. On the board or a transparency, write the above scoring system.

> - 1 point for each key word
> - 1 point for each Web site listing used (if the top selection that comes up for the search leads directly to the information, 1 point is given)
> - 1 point for each site visited

2. Inform students that you'll score yourself first. Using a computer, demonstrate how you try your key words from Part 1. (Be sure to try this out ahead of time so you are certain your key words will get you to the information as your first result!) You might also point out that putting quotes around phrases will contain and concentrate them even further, thereby yielding fewer and more accurate results.

3. Bring up your search engine and input your selected key words. Read the top resource and decide if you think it represents a reasonable site for locating the desired information. For example, using the sample search engine (Google.com) for the sample key words (*deadly volcanic eruption*), the top resource that comes up is (vulcan.wr.usgs.gov/LivingWith/VolcanicFacts/deadly_eruptions.html). It will take you to a chart that shows the most deadly eruptions ever recorded.

4. Demonstrate how you skim the material to see if you can find the answer to your question. Use headings, subheadings, and graphics when they are available. For this site, you'll immediately see a chart. Show students how you locate the chart entry for the deadliest eruption among those listed—an eruption in Tambora, Indonesia, in 1815 that killed 92,000 people. (Note: You might ask students if they're aware of the 2004 Thailand tsunami, which was even deadlier but which is not listed here because the death toll was caused indirectly by an offshore volcanic eruption, not directly by a volcano.)

5. Now compute your own points. The score for the sample is at right.

Key words (*deadly volcanic eruption*)	3 points
First source used	1 point
One site visited for information	1 point
Total	5 points

6. Organize students into the same partners or small groups from Part 1 and distribute their saved key words. Invite partners or groups, one at a time, to come forward to the computer and to follow your model as they attempt to answer their question. Record scores for each group and declare a winner(s).

TWO-PART LESSON: EVALUATING INTERNET PROPAGANDA

PART 1: GETTING THE "INFORMATION"

Explanation

Students need to develop consumer savvy in this age of technology. The wealth of immediately available information means that consumers themselves must be ready to ask analytic questions and be able to make judgments of validity and reliability. This is an enormous responsibility. This two-part lesson has students evaluate Web sites for propaganda that they'll confront often. Although the lessons focus specifically on discerning propaganda, the evaluative skills they teach can be used as the basis for additional lessons on Internet savvy—such as evaluating the worth of research sources. A healthy dose of skepticism is invaluable in dealing with the Internet! (See page 113 for a related lesson.)

Skill Focus

Generating and answering questions; classifying and categorizing; detecting bias, propaganda techniques, and exaggeration; establishing a purpose for reading; skimming and scanning

Materials & Resources

Text

* Articles from spoof Web sites (Used in this lesson: Save the Northwest Tree Octopus at zapatopi.net/treeoctopus.html)

Other

* For each student: photocopy of a printout of the selected spoof Web site article (or, if available, live Internet connections to these Web sites)

Prior to Lesson: Type in "spoof Web sites" in your search engine to locate articles on sites that are appropriate for your students. You'll find sites such as California's Velcro Crop (home.inreach.com/kumbach/velcro.html) and Save the Northwest Tree Octopus (zapatopi.net/treeoctopus.html). You'll see lots of strange articles that look authentic on every imaginable topic: male pregnancy, aluminum-foil deflector beanies to resist mind control, and so on. Of course, you'll need to sort through everything and decide what's appropriate for your students, but you will, we guarantee, encounter a great deal of silly stuff!

STEPS

1. Set up small groups or partners. Without providing any background about the purpose of this lesson or the accuracy of the day's text, distribute photocopies of the preselected article to students or have groups gather around a live Internet spoof Web site. (Note: Be sure to carefully monitor any live Internet work.) Write a few questions on the board to set a purpose for students' reading. For example, for the sample text, you might write:

    * Where does this species live?
    * How much time does this animal live out of the water?
    * What are its predators?
    * How does it help the ecosystem?
    * Should this animal be protected?

2. Instruct students to read the article. Have groups or partners discuss the questions.

3. Bring the groups back together to discuss the answers to this article. (Don't be surprised if your students have not yet questioned the validity of the topic.) Regardless of whether the information is challenged, hold a class discussion to consider all the answers.

4. Now write the word *valid* on the board. Tell the class that the lesson will continue tomorrow with an investigation. Close this Part of the lesson by saying something like, "We'll decide tomorrow how *valid* the information that we've learned about the tree octopus is." If some students have already begun to question and distrust the information, tell them that you hope they'll speak up tomorrow!

TWO-PART LESSON: EVALUATING INTERNET PROPAGANDA

PART 2: DEVELOPING THE CRITERIA

Explanation

This lesson, the second of two Parts, challenges students to think critically about the "information" they gathered in the previous lesson. As they work with four categories of critical criteria, students learn to evaluate Internet information and sources. (The four categories are based on the work of Robert Harris, 2000.) Learning not to believe everything they encounter—in print or on the Internet—is an invaluable lesson for all young readers.

Skill Focus

Generating and answering questions; classifying and categorizing; detecting bias, propaganda techniques, stereotypes, and exaggeration; establishing a purpose for reading; skimming and scanning for information

Materials & Resources

Text

- Articles from harmless spoof Web sites (Used in this lesson: Save the Northwest Tree Octopus at zapatopi.net/ treeoctopus.html)

Other

- Photocopies of the article used in Part 1 of this lesson or, if available, live Internet connection to the site (under supervision)

STEPS

1. Call attention to the word you wrote at the end of Part 1—*valid*. Invite a volunteer to look up the word in a collegiate dictionary and to read the definition aloud to the class. Hold a brief class discussion about the word's meaning and implications.

2. Have students gather in the same partners/groups formed for Part 1. Tell them that today they will evaluate the validity of the article they read and responded to in the previous lesson. Their task is to consider the article in terms of four different criteria. At the end of their group discussions, they should be prepared to present analyses and judgments to the whole class.

3. Write brief descriptions, one at a time, of the four categories on the board. Take time to define and discuss each category before proceeding to the next. After you discuss each category, present critical thinking questions to help students focus on the article they've read. Below is a list of the four categories, suggestions for discussion, and two critical thinking questions per category for the sample article used in this lesson. For your convenience, answers are provided in parentheses.

Credibility

Does the author or organization have good credentials?

Suggestion for discussion: You might relate this category to voters' considering the credentials of a mayoral or presidential candidate. What would those credentials be? What might make a voter trust the decisions a candidate would make in office?

How does this article try to establish its authority? (It includes links to credible, important-sounding organizations.)

What makes us question this site? (There are disclaimers about connections to some of the universities listed. The name of the organization is a play on words: "Greenpeas" instead of "Greenpeace.")

Accuracy

Does the article appear to be up-to-date and factual and to include details?

Suggestion for discussion: You might ask students how they sort through rumors that they hear and how they decide if a story—even a simple one—is true or untrue. What kinds of questions do they ask? Does it help them to know answers to the 5Ws and the H—*who, what, when, where, why,* and *how*? Ask them to reflect on how this kind of specificity helps to authenticate a story.

How does this article appear correct? (It is filled with details and scientific words and names and overall the information gives a very factual impression. There are lots of links and photos that seem to document the accuracy.)

What makes us question this site? (A few of the photos look staged and the octopus doesn't look real. Despite the fact that this Web site actually makes the information appear accurate, not all of the links work.)

Reasonableness

Do the contents of the article appear to be fair and truthful?

Suggestion for discussion: You might ask students how often they think people rely on their own "gut feelings" to decide if something is fair and truthful. Do students think this is a legitimate test? Or you might have them consider why people in line at the grocery store often pick up newspapers that proclaim ridiculous stories. What makes people spend money on absurd stories?

How does this article appear sensible? (Although we should be immediately skeptical of this article—because, after all, we do know that the octopus is a sea creature—the appearance of accuracy and credibility are strong enough that we may discount good sense.)

What makes us question this site? (Do you know anyone who has seen an octopus in a tree? If we stop for a moment to really think about it, this is a very silly idea! There is also an abundance of suspicious information, such as a list of other animals that the site suggests should be protected through legislation. Do the Mountain Walrus, the Manhattan Beach Mottled Roach, and the Rock Nest Monster really need protection? And is there actually a list of conservation organizations that includes People for the Ethical Treatment of Pumpkins?)

Support

Are sources and contact information available? Can we triangulate it?

Suggestion for discussion: Triangulate is a sophisticated but important word that can be defined for students by focusing on the prefix *tri* meaning "three." Help students realize that what this really means is: Can we prove the information by checking two additional sources for a total of three sources?

How does our article appear to be supported? (A large organization supposedly supports it, and there are links to other organizations that appear to be national or international.)

What makes us question this site? (If we use a search engine or any other resources, we won't be able to find any other information about or support for the existence of this species. Also, many of the links provided by this site don't respond.)

4. Provide sufficient time, perhaps spanning an additional day, for groups to gather, discuss the criteria, and evaluate the article. Bring the class back together so that each group can present findings.

5. Conclude the lesson by reminding students that although the Web site chosen for this exploration is harmless, spoof sites can be quite dangerous. For example, while appearing to represent legitimate credit card companies or banks, even incorporating well-known logos and trademarks, certain sites are committing fraud. You might sum up by saying something like, "The Internet holds many great possibilities for all of us, but it also harbors great dangers. This lesson should make us think—"We definitely can't believe everything we read or see!"

PREDICTIONS: CONFIRMED OR CONTRADICTED?

Explanation

Making predictions engages the reader in many other thinking activities, including questioning. Each time a reader makes a prediction, he or she is really formulating a question: Is this really what's going to turn out to be true? Good readers must also evaluate, during and after reading, whether their predictions have been confirmed or contradicted. This lesson focuses on making predictions from one chapter to another in a novel. It also provides practice with a graphic organizer as it engages students in all aspects of the key skill of making predictions.

Skill Focus

Making predictions about text; asking questions before and during reading; establishing a purpose for reading; using prior knowledge; using graphic organizers; clarifying main ideas and details

Materials & Resources

Text

- Any grade-appropriate chapter book of which students have already read at least a few chapters (Used in this lesson: Chapter 4 of *Island of the Blue Dolphins* by Scott O'Dell)

Other

- Photocopies, 1 for each student, of a prepared predictions chart (see Prior to the Lesson)

Prior to the Lesson: *Read through your selected material and jot down five or six statements that represent predictions a reader might legitimately make about the material. Change half of the statements to reflect incorrect predictions. Create a chart of all predictions. See diagram below for suggested form.*

STEPS

1. Remind students that good readers always ask themselves questions before and during reading. Some of the most important questions are in the form of predictions. Today's lesson will give students practice in both evaluating a set of predictions about a text and also in making their own predictions and then evaluating them.

2. Display the preselected chapter book (one that students are currently reading). Call students' attention to the material they have already read and provide the name of the next chapter.

3. Distribute a photocopy of the prepared chart to each student. Tell them to read through the list of predictions and to circle either "True" or "False" for each statement. An example chart for the sample text is below:

Prediction					Page #
The Aleuts will leave without paying.	True	False	Confirmed	Contradicted	
Chief Chowig, Karana's father, and his tribe will conquer the Aleuts.	True	False	Confirmed	Contradicted	
The Aleuts leave the island peacefully.	True	False	Confirmed	Contradicted	
Ulape, Karana's brother, will be killed by the Russians.	True	False	Confirmed	Contradicted	

4. Distribute copies of the text to students. As they read, they should check the accuracy of their predictions. Instruct them to circle whether their predictions have been confirmed or contradicted and to record the relevant page number in the final column.

5. Now have students share their findings. (Reassure students that an incorrect guess is fine, even expected, because that's what predictions are all about—taking best guesses that may or may not prove to be true.)

6. Follow up by having students create their own prediction charts for the next chapter. (You'll need to modify the model chart by eliminating the "True" and "False" column, but otherwise you can use this chart as a template.) Remind them to base their predictions on what they have already read in previous chapters.

WHY THIS BOOK AND NOT THAT ONE?

Explanation

Readers, including struggling readers, abandon books for many reasons. If we teach students how to understand the decision-making process that lies behind selecting a book, they will spend less time abandoning books and more time engaged in reading. In this lesson, students first have a chance to sort out their motivations by posing questions about why they are drawn to certain books, and then they get to actually choose new books to read.

Skill Focus

Establishing a purpose for reading; generating questions and answers; following multi-step directions; making predictions about text; identifying different type of genres

Materials & Resources

Text

- A variety of grade-appropriate books of varying lengths and genres, such as biographies, mysteries, science fiction, and informational books

Other

- Several tubs, pails, laundry baskets, etc. for displaying the books
- Chart paper and marker
- 1 index card for each student

Bonus Ideas

Think about setting up a box in your classroom labeled, "BOOKS NOT TO READ." Include in it books that individual students dislike. In the same way that students often want to read banned or challenged books, they may well be motivated to pick up what their peers condemned!

STEPS

1. Ask students to think about their reasons for choosing the books they do during library time, at home, or during silent reading. List their reasons on chart paper. Encourage them to formulate their reasons as questions, because making these decisions is actually a process of asking oneself a set of questions. Guide students, as needed, to come up with a list that includes reasons like the following:

    Reasons for Choosing a Good Book
    - Will this book make me laugh?
    - Did a friend with my same interests like this book?
    - Is this book about something I really want to learn?
    - Is this book in a genre I love (mystery, science fiction, etc.)?
    - Is the author one of my favorites?
    - Do the illustrations look interesting?
    - Does the summary on the back make the book sound exciting?

2. Now hold a class discussion about why students abandon books. Make this a safe environment by telling students that you, too, have sometimes abandoned books. Guide the discussion to help students analyze what lies behind their decision to stay with a book versus a decision to abandon it. Help students understand that by knowing their own likes and dislikes well enough to pick up a book that suits them, they will be less likely to give up on books they've started. This means they can devote more time to the actual enjoyment of reading! And in addition, if they scan through to check the length and read the first few pages to make sure they can understand the material, their book selection will be even more efficient and successful.

3. Place students into groups. Provide a tub of books for each group.

4. Instruct students to dig through the books to locate two or three that interest them. (Have students search the tub one a time—perhaps in alphabetical order—to avoid having two students select the same books.) Remind them to follow all the guidelines the class has just discussed.

5. When all students have chosen a few books, invite them to explain to their group their reasons for selecting a particular book.

6. Provide about 10 to 15 minutes for students to read one of the books they chose. Close by distributing an index card to each student. Instruct them to write, "I chose the book _____ because _____ _____." Requiring them to state their reasons explicitly should help them understand more fully the decision-making process.

RECOGNIZING THE SPEAKER

<table>
<tr><td>

Explanation

Determining the point of view of a narrative text should be among a reader's first questions in approaching a text. Authors choose the point of view that best fits the way they want to relate their tale. Students need to be made aware of the different points of view and how they can change a story. This lesson engages students in work with a pocket chart as they focus on pronouns expressing first-person point of view.

Skill Focus

Identifying speaker; determining person and point of view; coding text; establishing a purpose for reading; generating questions and answers

Materials & Resources

Text

• Multiple copies of a narrative text told from first-person point of view (Used in this lesson: *Lia's Journey* by Nancy J. Nielsen)

Other

• Prepared sentence strips; pocket chart

• Highlighter tape in 2 colors

• 6 VIP strips for each student: 3 in one color and 3 in another

Bonus Ideas

• You might open or close the lesson with songs that demonstrate different points of view. For example, "We Are Family" by Sister Sledge works well for first person and "Suds in the Bucket" by Sara Evans for third person.

</td><td>

Prior to the Lesson: From your preselected text, choose five or six sentences that clearly are written from the first-person point of view. Include at least one direct-address sentence that represents a lesser character's use of the main character's name. Write these sentences on pocket-chart sentence strips.

Note: This lesson works especially well if you follow it up with a lesson focused on third-person point of view. You can use the steps in this lesson with a third-person story. Focus for that lesson will be on these pronouns: he, she, it, him, hers, his, her, its, they, them, their, theirs.

STEPS

1. Tell students that as good readers pick up a book to read, they always ask themselves about the book's point of view. They want to know: Is this book told from the first-person or the third-person point of view?

2. Explain that when a story is told in first person, a character (almost always the main character) is speaking from his or her own point of view and uses certain pronouns to refer to himself or herself. On a transparency or the board, write the following pronouns and discuss them with students: *I, me, my, mine, we, us, our, ours.*

3. Display the text you'll be using. Depending upon your students' skill level, you might identify the book ahead of time as a first-person story or you might have students deduce its point of view as the lesson proceeds. Place one of the sentence strips in the pocket chart. Have students silently read the sentence and look for clues that indicate whether/why it's written from the first-person point of view. Have volunteers use highlighter tape to mark the appropriate pronouns. A set of sentences from the sample text, with relevant pronouns highlighted in light gray, is below:

    a. I was on my way out to the Navajo Reservation for the summer, maybe longer.

    b. My cousin Seth watched TV in one of them.

    c. Although Grams could speak Navajo, my mom had barely learned the language.

    d. "Give it time, Lia ," she said quietly on my first day.

    e. Grams was intent on teaching me all about my heritage.

4. Once you've fully established that this is a first-person story, tell students that one (or two) sentence(s) includes something else special that you want to discuss. Explain that in a first-person story, readers typically discover the name of the main character/narrator by noting how other characters address him or her. Have a volunteer highlight the narrator's name in the displayed sentences. (In the list above, the name is shaded in darker gray.)

5. Next, distribute a copy of the text, along with three VIP strips in one color and three in a second color, to each student. Instruct students to read until they've placed three strips of one color on pronouns that indicate first-person point of view and three strips of the second color to mark information that reveals the narrator's name.

</td></tr>
</table>

WHAT'S THE AUTHOR'S PURPOSE?

Explanation

In this lesson students focus on a key question that all readers must ask: Why did the author write this piece? What was his or her purpose? After learning the three major purposes—to inform, to entertain, or to persuade—students sort different genres and texts. First by categorizing index cards and then by analyzing different text selections, students make informed choices among the three author purposes.

Skill Focus

Analyzing author's purpose; reading and navigating Internet and media text; making predictions about text; using graphic organizers; classifying and categorizing ideas; responding to text through a variety of methods

Materials & Resources

Text
- For modeling: 3 brief text selections, each representing one of the 3 major author purposes
- For student work: Snipped newspaper and magazine articles, photocopied poems and short stories, snipped newspaper comics, brochures, or any other appropriate consumable text

Other
- 30 or more index cards
- Tape and/or glue sticks
- 3 large pieces of butcher paper

Bonus Ideas

The three charts created during this lesson would make a great classroom or hallway display!

Prior to the Lesson: Assemble at least 30 index cards. On each card write one word or phrase that describes a type of text or genre. See the list at right for examples. (Examples are clustered by author purpose for your convenience.)

Note: Although we have not broken this lesson into parts, it will probably work best as a multiday lesson.

Inform
- biography
- chart
- graph
- how-to
- math book
- science book
- history book
- autobiography
- directions
- recipe

- fantasy
- horror
- western
- science fiction
- myth
- legend

Persuade
- billboard
- bumper sticker
- TV commercial
- advertisement
- radio commercial
- travel brochure
- campaign speech

Entertain
- mystery
- fairy tale
- comics
- poetry

STEPS

1. Tell students that good readers always ask themselves why the author might have written a particular text. Explain that there are three major purposes that motivate authors to write: to inform, to entertain, or to persuade. Display and read aloud the three preselected texts and model for students how you identify the author's purpose for each.

2. Now mount three pieces of butcher paper on your chalkboard. Title the first sheet "Inform," the second "Entertain," and the third "Persuade."

3. Organize students into three or four small groups. Distribute an equal number of randomly shuffled index cards to each group. Instruct group members to work together to divide their stack of cards into three sets that represent the three main categories discussed in Steps 1 and 2.

4. Call on a student from each group to come forward with that group's sets and to identify which category each set represents. Read aloud the individual cards in each set. As you read each card, work with students to evaluate whether it's in the correct category. With students' help, tape all index cards onto the correct charts.

5. Now distribute a text piece to each student. Instruct students to read the selection and to pay close attention to the author's purpose. Remind them the text will fall into a genre and also into one of the three categories.

6. Next, have students, one at a time, bring their text to the front of the class. Ask each student the following questions: "What type of writing/genre did you read?" and "What was the author's purpose for writing this particular text?"

7. As students answer correctly, invite them to glue their text to the appropriate chart. Continue until all students have come forward.

Using Graphic and Semantic Organizers

Graphic and semantic organizers—diagrams or pictorial representations that visually illustrate concepts and relationships—play an essential role in building students' reading comprehension. Adaptable for use with just about any kind of fiction or nonfiction text, they make vague and abstract ideas concrete so that students can more easily process and understand these concepts. For example, illustrating the workings of government (a common topic in grades 4 to 6) via a network of hierarchical boxes and connecting lines can be far more effective than merely having students read about them.

The National Reading Panel reports that these tools have a positive impact on three specific areas of learning:

1. They help students focus on text structure while reading.

2. They provide a framework that visually represents textual relationships.

3. They facilitate students' writing well-organized summaries. (NRPR; NICHHD, 2000)

The National Reading Panel research also says that "teaching students to use a systematic, visual graphic to organize the ideas that they are reading about develops the ability of the students to remember what they read and may transfer in general to better comprehension and achievement in social studies and science content areas" (NRPR; NICHHD, p. 4-75).

Furthermore, extensive research into concept mapping (Novak, 1991) and thinking maps (Hyerle, 1996) has proven that visual maps help learners understand the concepts of similarities and differences, cause and effect, part as opposed to whole, and analogical sets. Understanding these types of relationships is an essential component of conceptual change and cognitive growth (Brooks, 2004).

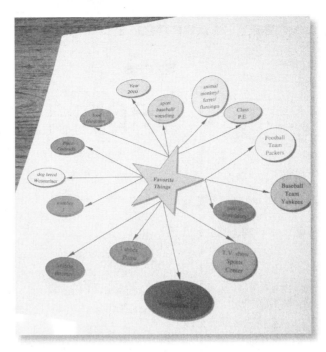

This graphic organizer was created by a student learning to use the computer to map concepts.

For these authors, and others in past generations, the closest experience to using true graphic organizers was the venerable exercise of diagramming sentences. The sentence diagram (which offered a means of picturing the technical aspects of sentence construction) can even be seen as a precursor to today's graphic organizers. Many students may have huffed and grunted, "Why are we doing this?" but in the end, relationships among sentence parts were distilled and represented in a uniquely clear way. Some of us may hate to admit it, but we actually enjoyed this puzzle of lines! We are not advocating going back to sentence-diagramming days, but realizing the strengths of this approach can help us better grasp the valuable role of all graphics in literacy instruction. Indeed, such graphics can be the key for some students—especially those who are visual learners—in achieving comprehension of many abstract concepts.

Although there are countless versions of organizers available, the research of Bromley, Irwin-De Vitis, and Modlo (1995) suggests that there are four basic structures from which all graphic and semantic organizers evolve: conceptual, hierarchical, cyclical, and sequential. In the lessons in this section, you will find examples of all four structures.

While younger students focus on learning in more kinesthetic and tactile ways, by the time children are in the upper grades they need to be challenged with more complex ways of looking at concepts. In these lessons, they learn to use the concept mapping technique to break a main topic into categorical parts; they investigate parts of the book to create hierarchical organizers; they look at such literary devices as "circular plot" when completing cyclical organizers; and they learn to take careful notes (a crucial skill they'll use through college and beyond) while doing sequencing and compare/contrast activities.

All of these visual-mapping approaches are important classroom activities because they guide students in building organizing frameworks for their thinking (Ausubel, Novak, & Hanesian, 1978). They're also a lot of fun, so enjoy as you and your students engage in learning through graphic and semantic organizers!

CONCEPT MAPPING TO IMPROVE COMPREHENSION

Explanation

Concept maps are used to help students delve deeper into an idea, theme, or topic contained in text. They generally start with a central idea and explore its facts, details, and descriptions to develop a clearer understanding of the main topic. This lesson will help students organize and manage expository text they are reading.

Skill Focus

Identifying main plot events; paraphrasing and summarizing using main ideas and details; categorizing aspects of the main topic

Materials & Resources

Text

- An informational text (Used in this lesson: *When Marian Sang* by Pam Muñoz Ryan)

- Content area textbook, such as a science or social studies text

Other

- Chalkboard or butcher paper stretched across a wall

- Colored pencils or markers

- Pictures gathered from magazines or from the Internet

Bonus Ideas

Try assigning to small groups different chapters/sections of a content unit that you're about to study. Let each group read and map out their chapter. Allow time for them to come up and add their map to a general mapping of the topic. Then, invite each group to teach their chapter to the class based on what they've included on their particular branch.

STEPS

1. Read aloud the preselected book. Explain to students that they will be using a technique called "concept mapping" to explore the different aspects of the main topic. For the sample book, the main topic is the life of a famous person, Marian Anderson.

2. On the chalkboard or a large piece of butcher paper, draw a silhouette and write the main topic ("Marian Anderson") at the center. Now explain you'll be brainstorming about different categories that were presented in the book. For the sample book, these categories include Influences in Early Life, Culture of the Times, Life in Her 20s, Influences in Young Adult Life, and Return to the U.S. Tell students they'll want to eliminate some categories by combining them with other, very similar ones (e.g., Life in Her 20s can be part of Influences in Young Adult Life).

3. Add the major categories as branches from the central topic. Organize students into small groups and assign each group a branch of the concept map. Discuss what images might best portray the categories. You might either have students sketch something or find illustrations. For example, for the sample book, Influences in Early Life might be illustrated by a young girl singing and Influences in Young Adult Life by an "Audition" sign. Tape the images next to the relevant categories to add greater visual interest.

4. Now, focus on one of the categories to model how details can be added to the map. Be sure to use words and phrases, not sentences, as shown below:

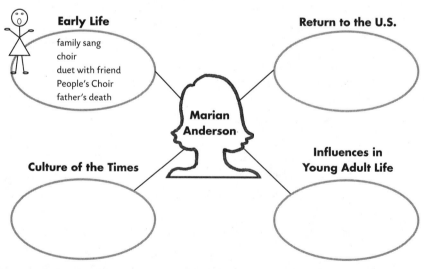

5. Have groups follow your model, completing their branch by using details and descriptions from the text. Review the concept map upon conclusion. Have each group choose a representative to present their portion of the map to the class.

HIERARCHICAL ORGANIZERS

STEPS

1. Give students a quick and easy explanation of a hierarchy. Tell them a hierarchy is much like a ladder system or a chain of command—something is at the top and there are levels represented below.

2. You might offer a quick sketch of a hierarchical organizer that represents the categories of your own school. Elicit students' input as you create a simple hierarchical map that starts at the top with the principal. One possible example follows:

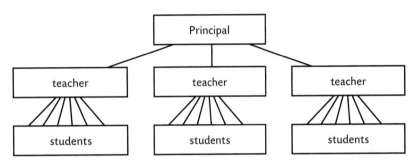

3. Now tell students that the map that you'll all work on together is a hierarchical system that you use almost every day. Open the table of contents for the sample text and explain to students that this is a hierarchical system—it begins with a major concept or idea that guides the entire book, moves to units that offer subdivisions of the material, then to chapters that provide the next level of detail, and, finally, to lessons or subheadings that divide the chapter into digestible portions.

4. On an index card, write the top level of the hierarchy, which in this case would be the topic of the book. For example, using the sample book, the top level would be: "Early United States History." Write a small "#1" on the top of the card and place this index card at the top of your pocket chart.

5. Tell students there are eight units of study that represent the next level. On a card, record the first unit: "Ancient Americans." Make a small "#2" (for second level) and place this card far to the left on the level under the top card. Tell students that seven other cards belong on this row but that you'll only follow one strand for now.

6. On the third level under "Ancient Americans," show students how the topic branches again into two chapters, which you will record: "First Americans" and "Indians of North America." Write these on two separate cards and file them on the third level of the pocket chart under the unit title, marking each card with a small "#3."

○ **Bonus Ideas**

Have students experiment by using coat hangers, string, and index cards to build hierarchical maps. These "hanging maps" can decorate your classroom and remind students how to apply this system of organization. Have students write the topic of the map on both sides of one index card and tape it so that it fills the center space of the wire hanger. Then they can hole punch the top center of each index card needed for the next level of the hierarchy. Help them write a targeted word for that level on both sides of an index card. Thread string through the hole and tie one end to the card and one to the bottom of the coat hanger so that the card dangles. Do this for as many cards as there are categories at that level of the hierarchy. Follow the same procedure for the next level of the hierarchy, attaching those cards to the bottoms of the dangling index cards. You and your students now have a mobile representing a hierarchical structure, ready to hang anywhere in your classroom!

7. From here, drop down another level. This level will have branches leading to three lessons under "First Americans" and five lessons under "Indians of North America." Write the titles on their respective cards and mark each with "#4."

8. Clarify any questions that students have about this hierarchy.

9. Now, organize students into the same number of groups for the number of remaining units to be completed. Give each group a stack of about 20 cards and a marker. Tell them they'll be replicating what you've just modeled, following a strand through to the fourth level, though they will start with the name of the unit (the second level), as the main topic is the same in all cases.

10. Once everyone has finished, clear a large space on the floor of the classroom and tape down the butcher paper. Remove your cards from the pocket chart and start building the hierarchical chart of the table of contents on the floor. Let each group come up and construct their portion when called upon.

11. At the conclusion, tell students they have helped to create what is perhaps the "world's largest" hierarchical chart! During the next class period, invite them to work on another text in small groups.

CYCLICAL GRAPHIC ORGANIZERS

Prior to the Lesson: Use the sample organizer on page 62 as a model to create a cyclical organizer template. Make photocopies for students.

STEPS

1. Review with students the definition of a cycle (something that goes through various stages and comes back to its beginning point, only to start again) and ask them to name some common cycles. Some possibilities are: life cycle of a moth or a frog, cycle of the seasons, time and calendar cycles, water cycle, daily cycle, and song cycle. Prompt them with a couple of straightforward examples of cycles if necessary.

2. Begin sketching out the water cycle, telling students they'll be helping you figure out its stages. (See diagram on page 62.) Start by drawing the ground, with groundwater flowing underneath it.

3. Ask students, "What happens next?" They should say something like, "It flows underground until it reaches a body of water, then merges with that." Draw an arrow pointing to this next stage. Label it "lake or stream."

4. Now ask students, "What happens next?" Help them, as needed, to describe the step of transpiration/evaporation. Draw an arrow pointing to the sun, and label it "transpiration." Ask students, "What happens next?" Helps students describe this stage as "water vapor." They might say something like, "Moisture rises as warm vapor from the water and gathers in the atmosphere in the form of clouds." Draw an arrow pointing to a cloud. Ask students, "What happens next?"

5. Students will likely identify rain or snow. Draw an arrow to this next stage and label it "precipitation." Complete the cycle by drawing the last arrow to the ground and labeling it "infiltration." Ask students what has happened in this last stage, and point out that they are now back at the first stage in the cycle.

6. After you've checked that students understand what you've just gone through with the water cycle, introduce the sample text and tell students they will now be reading a story that uses a circular plot. Ask students to predict what a circular plot might be. Explain that circular plots follow a "rounded" pattern. Tell them a circular plot is similar to a water cycle, with one scene following another until it eventually returns to the beginning scene.

7. Now write the following question on the board, "What do I think might happen next?" Tell the students to read the story. As they read, tell students to be thinking about this question the entire time.

Explanation

Cyclical organizers can be used to illustrate everything from simple cycles to more complex cycles that require greater conceptual and logical reasoning. Many cycles discussed in classrooms focus on informational texts; this lesson takes a literary turn by focusing on fiction texts with circular plots. Using a circular plot is a great way to introduce predictions. Students fill out their graphic organizers by asking themselves, "What do I think might happen next?"

Skill Focus

Using graphic organizers to show organization of the text (cyclical); coding text; clarifying main ideas and details; identifying main events; creating outlines, notes, and diagrams to summarize

Materials & Resources

Text

- Any grade-appropriate narrative text that follows a cyclical pattern (Used in this lesson: *The Relatives Came* by Cynthia Rylant; alternate suggestions: *The Sunsets of Miss Olivia Wiggins* by Lester L. Laminack or *What About Me?* by Ed Young)

Other

- Chart paper
- Several VIP strips for each student
- 1 copy for each student of a cyclical organizer (see Prior to the Lesson)

Bonus Ideas

Bring in or have the students bring in appropriate songs that contain a cycle. For example, they might enjoy one with a circular plot. Have students listen for the cycle. As they listen they should jot notes in their cyclical organizer. When the song ends, have students form partners and share the notes they made on their graphic organizers.

8. Tell students that each time they come to a new scene, they should place a VIP strip directly at that point in the text. Have them continue this process until they have finished reading the story. For example, the sample story begins as the relatives all pile into an old station wagon and head up from Virginia. While at their relatives' house, they hug, laugh, hug some more, have a big supper, and sleep. They stay for several weeks. When it's time to leave, they load up the station wagon again and head back to Virginia. They are all very sad and miss each other — but not for long, because they all know it will happen again next summer!

9. Distribute a photocopy of a cyclical organizer to each student. When students have finished placing their strips, have them go back and reread a small portion of the text near which they have placed the VIP strips, then correctly fill out their cyclical organizer. Be sure they follow your model to include both sketches and labels.

10. After students have finished filling out their organizers, discuss the components of their cyclical graphs.

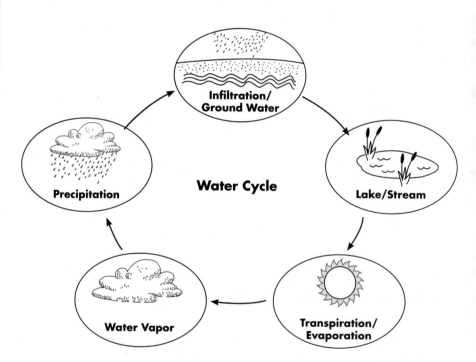

SEQUENTIAL LOGS

STEPS

1. Explain to students that today you will be doing a read-aloud and think-aloud with a text that has a clear and compelling sequence of events. Have them bring their pencils and gather with you in the read-aloud area.

2. Distribute one index card to each student. Tell them they are going to jot down important events as you read aloud and think aloud about the text. This process is illustrated for the sample book below:

Teacher's Read-Aloud	Teacher's Think-Aloud at Marked Places in Text
(1) Read the first page of text that describes how the speaker cannot remember his mother's or father's face, but can recall their love. Stop and share your comment. (2) Continue reading the story. Stop and make your observation just after the father hands his son the harmonica. (3) Continue reading and stop again to think aloud just after you read about how the family can hear a war raging outside their apartment, a war that nonetheless leaves them "untouched." (4) Continue until you've read about how the Nazis find the family. (5) Follow a similar procedure until you have completed the book, having students jot down notes on their own as you read and pause periodically.	(1)"This is very interesting. I wonder why he cannot remember his father's or mother's face. They must have passed away. I don't think you should take a note just yet, because he says he remembers their love, enfolding as a song. This leads me to believe, he is going to tell us more about his parents. I will continue to read." (2) "I think this is an important event, because not only is this the title of the book, but it is also a gift of music, which is very important to his family. Boys and girls, jot a quick note about his father giving him a harmonica." (3) "This could be an important event or note to take, a war raging, but he said they were left untouched, so I think we should wait to see what happens." (4) "Now I think you should take a note, because they were found by the Nazi soldiers." [Check to make sure that students understand what the reference to Nazi soldiers means.] (5) [Students continue taking notes about important events.]

3. Display the transparency of the Sequential Log. Discuss with students which events are the most important and which ones should come first, second, third, and so on. Fill in the transparency accordingly.

4. Distribute to each student a photocopy of the Sequential Log (Appendix, p. 121) and another index card. Tell students they will be reading another text on their own and taking notes as they read. To help them find a clear sequence of events, you may want to tell them to stop after each page, jot down two important events from that page, and then continue to read. Students should do this until the assigned reading is complete.

5. Now have students look at their index card and determine the six most important events, then write those in the correct order on their Sequential Log.

Explanation

Teaching students to listen and read for sequence greatly enhances overall comprehension. In this lesson, the teacher guides students by demonstrating the internal monologue they should have when reading a text to determine sequence. A thematically related text is then assigned so that students can undertake this process themselves and write down the sequence of events in a story.

Skill Focus

Using graphic organizers to show organization of text (sequential); rereading; creating notes and using internal organization; paraphrasing using main ideas, details, and events

Materials & Resources

Text

- Any grade-appropriate text that has a clear sequence of events (Used in this lesson: *The Harmonica* by Tony Johnston)

- An additional text with a clear sequence of events for your assigned reading selection

Other

- Sequential Log (see Appendix, p. 121), 1 copy for each student

- Transparency of Sequential Log for overhead

- Index cards, 2 for each student

Bonus Ideas

Partner students. Have students cut out the boxes from their completed Sequential Log. Then, ask them to trade their six pieces with the other partner and have students put the partner's pieces in order.

COMPARING/CONTRASTING TALES FROM DIFFERENT CULTURES USING A MATRIX

Explanation

When students compare and contrast key elements of stories, they can better understand plot, character, and setting. Students also see there is more than one way to tell a story, and, perhaps, may even be inspired to come up with their own creative versions of well-known tales! But they need a manageable and organized way to go about it, as they can get weighed down with lots of information when attempting to compare several tales. In this lesson, students use a matrix that allows them to neatly compare and contrast stories. They'll also get a kick out of hearing a very familiar fairy tale with "strange" twists set in very unfamiliar settings!

Skill Focus

Reading tales from different cultures to compare/contrast literary elements; using a graphic organizer (matrix); identifying main events; paraphrasing and summarizing using main ideas, events, details, and themes

Materials & Resources

Text

- Any grade-appropriate or easier version of the same story from different cultures (See Prior to the Lesson)

Other

- Compare/Contrast Matrix (see Appendix, p. 122), 1 for each student

- Transparency of the Compare/ Contrast Matrix

- Versions of the same story from different cultures (3–5 copies of each)

Prior to the Lesson: Make sure your class has a thorough understanding of the original Cinderella story. Although most students are familiar with the French version of "Cinderella" by Charles Perrault, they are probably not aware of other versions. Thus, over a period of days, read several versions of the Cinderella story (excluding the ones you chose for this lesson). While introducing these to the class, discuss similarities and differences among the characters, settings, illustrations, plots, and so on. Here are some alternate versions of the Cinderella story: The Irish Cinderlad, The Egyptian Cinderella, *and* The Korean Cinderella *by Shirley Climo;* Yeh-Shen: A Cinderella Story from China *by Ai-Ling Louie;* The Golden Slipper: A Vietnamese Legend *by Darrell Lum;* Mufaro's Beautiful Daughters: An African Tale *by John Steptoe;* Cendrillon: A Caribbean Cinderella *by Robert D. San Souci;* The Rough-Face Girl *by Rafe Martin.*

STEPS

1. Begin this lesson by reminding students of the Cinderella stories you've recently read aloud. Guide students as they review the similarities and differences in these previously read Cinderella stories.

2. Display a transparency of the Compare/Contrast Matrix and distribute a copy of this organizer (Appendix, p. 122) to each student. Using the original version of "Cinderella" by Charles Perrault, model how you take simplistic notes in the first row of boxes and have students fill out the first row on their copies. You may need to refer to the story, so be prepared with a copy of the book at hand.

3. Now, place students into groups of four or five, giving each group a different version of the Cinderella story. As they read, they should take notes in the second row of the matrix. After each page, students should discuss similarities and differences between the original version and the version they are reading.

4. Next, set up partners by pairing a student from one group with a student from a different group. Have each student give a quick summary of his or her book, describing the similarities and differences from the original version.

5. Repeat this lesson, assigning student groups a different version of the book on the second day. Have them fill out the third row of the matrix, comparing and contrasting with the original version. Collect the matrixes to check for understanding.

Creating and Using Images

Have you ever loved a book and then ventured to the theater expecting to enjoy it even more because of the added dimensions of sight and sound—only to be sorely disappointed that the movie doesn't meet your expectations? This phenomenon may be explained by the fact that good readers visualize what they're reading as they read. As good readers, we've already seen the play or movie in our mind's eye. We've held our own casting of characters, sometimes using people we know or stars we admire. We're already used our own props to establish the setting; we've called on numerous personal experiences and preferences to enrich our understanding of the plot. Then, we see what a Hollywood producer has envisioned for us—and so often it just doesn't match. And, not surprisingly, we like our version better! Most likely, without even consciously realizing it, we've been making use of a sophisticated, essential reading skill—the ability to form images based in part on connections we've made between our own experiences and the text we're reading.

This ability not only makes reading more enjoyable, it enables readers to grow as learners. The research of Gambrell and Koskinen (2002) suggests that there are two great advantages to creating and using mental images when reading: 1) images provide a framework, or "pegs," for organizing and remembering information from texts; and 2) mental images help integrate information across texts. To further understand the importance of creating images in reading, let's peek inside a classroom at look at how a student approaches visualizing.

Jeff and Kenny are in "The Reading Zone," a comfortable reading area in a fifth-grade classroom, furnished with beanbag chairs, cushions, and lots of varied reading materials. They've both chosen different magazines to read. Absorbed in his article about fishing, Kenny is interrupted by Jeff, who wants to share something he's reading.

"Hey, I really like the way this article starts," Jeff says as he begins to read aloud to his friend. "It says, 'They look like aliens from a Star Wars movie. They wear body armor from their shoulders down to their shins. Thick pads shield their chests, hips, arms, and legs. The special gloves they wear have padding on each finger. On their heads, they display space-age helmets designed to protect the face as well as the head....'"

Kenny listens to and understands all the words he hears, but they don't conjure up a picture that is familiar to him. He imagines space-age astronauts at first, but decides (from what he has seen on television) that they wouldn't have shields on only their chests, hips, arms, and legs. While Kenny's still attempting to make sense of the words, Jeff continues to read about the off-beat characters who wear these suits. Then, he mentions racing 60 miles an hour downhill, making split-second decisions, and a character who has had more cracked ribs than she can count. Kenny searches his mind, but still doesn't grasp what the text is saying.

Finally, without wanting to admit that he's in the dark, Kenny asks if the article includes a picture. Jeff shows him a photograph that helps to fill in some gaps. Using the title, "Extreme Biking," and seeing the picture of a padded biker wearing a helmet and soaring down a mountainside, Kenny figures out that his imagined astronaut is in fact a mountain biker.

Although Kenny has struggled for understanding, he is actually far more fortunate than many other students. He may lack the background information needed to create the appropriate image, but he brings several strengths to the situation: He realizes that he *should* be picturing what he's learning/reading; he actively incorporates new information as it is supplied; and he is willing to shift images in an attempt to understand. Many students do not bring these abilities and strategies to their reading; this lack of awareness puts them at a great disadvantage in their reading.

The lessons in this section are aimed at helping teachers help students whose imaging skills range from rudimentary to well-developed. Imagery training has long proven successful as a way to improve students' memory and inferential reasoning about written text (Levin & Divine-Hawkins, 1974; Borduin, Borduin, & Manley, 1994). You'll find lessons here on many different aspects of visualizing—from telling stories through illustrations to using similes and metaphors to create "mind pictures" to playing games with symbolism (and identifying it in literature). So, as we begin this section, let your "good reader" camera roll. We believe you'll gain some unique ideas for teaching your students to *see* what they read so that they can better comprehend it.

The images in a text provide a framework, or "pegs," for a reader to organize and remember information.

SIMILES AND METAPHORS: WHISPERS AND SHOUTS

Explanation

Similes and metaphors in narrative text have the power to transform a dull or ordinary piece of writing into a flight of fancy, a revelation, a trip to another world. The images conjured by similes and metaphors can be so powerful as to stick with a reader for years. Identifying similes and metaphors in text, and understanding their use, greatly helps students get what the author is trying to convey, which, after all, is the ultimate goal for teachers of reading.

Skill Focus

Identifying similes and metaphors in text; creating mental images; coding text; clarifying main ideas and details; using word knowledge and context clues

Materials & Resources

Text

- Any grade-appropriate book, newspaper, or magazine that contains multiple similes and metaphors (Used in this lesson: *Holes* by Louis Sachar)

Other

- Overhead or chart paper
- Several VIP strips for each child

Bonus Ideas

Students might illustrate an example of a simile or metaphor they locate in the text. This could be quite humorous. For example, for the sample text simile, a student could draw a girl replacing her head with an empty flower pot. Or for the metaphor in Step 1, "Jordan is a dictionary," students could draw a dictionary with human features, such as arms, legs, hair, eyes, and so on.

STEPS

1. Discuss with students that authors use similes and metaphors to help readers create mental images or pictures through comparisons. Explain that students might think of similes as *whispers* because when they compare, they use *like* or *as*. For example, "Jordan is as sweet as a Jolly Rancher." On the other hand, we might think of metaphors as *shouts* because they say something IS something else. For example, "Jordan is a dictionary."

2. Give students a few minutes to discuss the difference between similes and metaphors and to come up with several similes and metaphors as a class. Be ready to prompt students with a few more evocative examples of similes and metaphors if necessary.

3. Next, read an excerpt that contains similes or metaphors. Below is an example from the sample text, along with a model think-aloud:

Sample Text to Read Aloud	Teacher's Think-Aloud at Marked Places in Text
Myra's head is as empty as a flowerpot.	"What things are being compared?" (Myra's head and a flowerpot) "What does the author mean by saying that Myra's head is as empty as a flowerpot?" (She's not very smart.) "Using *as* in the comparison makes this statement a simile. I will tear off one of my VIP strips with an *S* at the top, and on it I will write the two things being compared: Myra's head and flowerpot."

4. Next, have students prepare one set of VIP strips by cutting a sticky note into six strips and writing an S at the top of three and an M at the top of the other three. Explain to students that they will be using these strips— S standing for simile and M for metaphor—to mark places in the sample text where they find examples of similes and metaphors.

5. Now have students read the preselected text, locating similes and metaphors. Instruct them to write the two things being compared on the strip before placing it in the text. Circulate about the room, checking informally on students' work and offering guidance as needed.

6. Call up a pair of students to the board and ask one student to read the two words written on either an S or an M strip. As the student reads, the other student should write the words on the chalkboard. Then, ask someone in the class to identify that metaphor or simile from the text. Finally, have another student (or two) explain what it means in his or her own words.

SKETCHING AN IMAGE

Explanation

Creating images in our minds when listening to or reading a text, whether it comes naturally or is teacher-directed, has powerful effects on comprehension. It allows us to make predictions about text, to better remember the story being told, and, of course, to associate more meaning with what's being read. In this lesson, students sketch their images, compare them with both peers' and the original illustrator's, and analyze differences.

Skill Focus

Explaining effects of imagery in a variety of texts; making predictions about text; using mental images; responding to texts through a variety of methods; rereading to find details

Materials & Resources

Text

- Multiple copies of a text with illustrations and vivid word usage

Other

- Black construction paper; markers

- Removable/painters' tape (usually purple)

- Sheet of unlined paper, 1 for each student

Bonus Ideas

Cover up a book illustration and place the book in a large, sealed baggie. Tack it in the middle of a bulletin board. Title it "What do you see when you read the author's words?" Have students come to the bulletin board on an individual basis, read the text, and sketch an illustration for the covered-up picture. Post all students' sketches.

Prior to the Lesson: Cut out a piece of black construction paper and use removable tape to place it over a picture in your preselected text.

STEPS

1. Reiterate that creating mental images allows text to come to life for readers. Discuss how students will both better understand and remember a piece when they try to picture what the author is saying. Tell them that in today's lesson they will have the opportunity to see how their own images compare to other students' and to the illustrator's.

2. Explain that even when a book includes pictures, creating your own images as you read is important. It helps your memory as well as your understanding of what you've read. You value the author's words more when you use them to create your own images.

3. Distribute a sheet of paper to each student. Instruct students to close their eyes. Invite them to create a mental image as you read a preselected poem or excerpt from a narrative text. Allow a few minutes for students to sketch what they visualized.

4. Have students compare and contrast their sketches with one or two others (sitting across the aisle or table from them). Then, reveal the picture from the book. Discuss that all readers have their own picture in their mind, and that some may focus more on one element while others focus on another.

5. Distribute a copy of the preselected text to each student. Explain that you have covered up an illustration in the selection. Remind students that the picture is covered up for a reason: They are to be trustworthy and they are not to peek underneath! When they come to the covered picture, they are to continue to read and build mental images.

6. After students finish the selection, have them go back to the covered picture and reread the surrounding text. Tell them to sketch what they think is under the black construction paper. Once their sketches are finished and if time allows, they may add color to the picture.

7. Have the entire class carefully pull up the tape and reveal the text's picture at the same time.

8. Walk around and check to see how close students' drawings are to the original illustration. Then, have students discuss the similarities and differences between their sketches and the illustrator's. Invite students to explain why they think their pictures were so similar to or so different from the picture in the book.

CREATING MENTAL IMAGES: PICTURE THAT!

STEPS

1. Discuss with students that authors use vivid words to help readers create mental images or pictures in their minds. This vivid language may call upon one or several of a reader's five senses. Good readers not only focus on these words to create mind pictures, they are also aware of which senses they are using to form the images.

2. Without displaying any illustrations, begin to read aloud a particularly vivid portion of the preselected text. Once you have read a few sentences or a paragraph, have students turn to a partner and discuss what they pictured and which senses they called upon to form their image. How did the author's language help them visualize?

3. Show students the relevant book illustration. Have them discuss whether the picture in their mind was similar to the one in the book. How did the illustrator interpret the author's language?

4. Now display the transparency of the Creating Mental Images organizer (Appendix, p. 123). Read another passage from the book. Invite a volunteer to come forward to make a quick sketch in one of the boxes of the mental image he or she formed. Jot down a few words from the passage and the corresponding page number. Then have the student fill in which sense(s) he or she used.

5. Set up partners. Distribute a copy of the text and of the organizer to each pair. Instruct students to read further in the text and to follow the modeled procedure to complete the organizer.

6. Have partners share their final products with the whole class. Encourage discussion of similarities and differences in the various images, of how the author's language helped students create the images, and of the senses they called upon.

Explanation

In this lesson students are asked to focus on two critical aspects of how readers visualize. They note authors' use of vivid language and they pay attention to which of their five senses that language calls upon. Then they fill out an organizer that helps them make sense of all of that information!

Skill Focus

Creating mental images to aid comprehension; explaining the effects of imagery in a variety of texts; using graphic organizers; using repair strategies (visualization)

Materials & Resources

Text

- Multiple copies of a grade-appropriate illustrated text that has vivid word usage

Other

- Transparency of Creating Mental Images organizer (see Appendix, p. 123)

- 1 copy for each partner set of same organizer

Bonus Ideas

Have partners locate a book or story they have already read. Allot about five minutes for one partner to skim through, locate a text section that uses vivid words, and read it aloud. The other partner should listen and then describe the image created in his/her mind. Only at this point should the reader share any illustration that accompanies his/her chosen section. Then partners should switch roles.

FIGURATIVE LANGUAGE: IDIOMS

Explanation

Reading books that highlight and/or use a lot of idioms is a great way both to generate interest in words and to help students practice conjuring images while reading. This lesson focuses on teaching students how to better comprehend text by understanding figurative language, especially idioms.

Skill Focus

Applying knowledge of figurative language; creating mental images to aid comprehension; using graphic organizers; responding to texts through a variety of methods; explaining the effects of imagery

Materials & Resources

Text

- Any grade-appropriate text that includes multiple idioms (Suggested for this lesson: *Punching the Clock: Funny Action Idioms* by Marvin Terban or *In a Pickle and Other Funny Idioms* by Marvin Terban)

Other

- Sentence strips (see "Prior to the Lesson")

- Pocket chart

- 1 sheet of unlined paper for each student

- Colored pencils or thin-tip markers

Bonus Ideas

Here's a twist on traditional Charades—"Idiom Charades." With students' help, compile a list of idioms and write them on sticky notes. Place them in a basket. In turn, have students draw one out of the basket to act out.

Prior to the Lesson: To get students into the spirit of idioms, read aloud from a couple of books that use vivid, funny idioms—for example, you might use Tedd Arnold's Parts, More Parts, *or* Even More Parts, *which highlight body parts. Also, prepare sentence strips; each should contain an idiom that is (ideally) already familiar to your students. A list of sample idioms is at right.*

it's a piece of cake
beat around the bush
bite off more than you can chew
break someone's heart
catch some Z's
he's a couch potato
zip your lip!
make a mountain out of a mole hill

STEPS

1. Tell students that idioms are exaggerated, sometimes outlandish expressions that are used to emphasize a point by conjuring a vivid image in the listener's mind. Explain that idioms are phrases that cannot be understood literally and that all elements of the phrase don't necessarily translate directly. Good readers know that understanding the meaning of idioms will help them better comprehend text.

2. Display the prepared sentence strips, one by one. Ask students if they know what each phrase means. Check, too, to see if students can use each phrase correctly in a sentence. Help students as needed and place each strip in the pocket chart.

3. Now divide the class into small groups—one for each section or chapter of the preselected text—and assign each group a segment. Distribute a plain sheet of paper to each student.

4. Have students fold their paper in half vertically, then in half two more times. When they open their paper and hold it horizontally, there should be four columns and two rows, as shown at right.

5. Explain to students that they should first read their segment of the book silently. (There's bound to be some giggling!) Have them go back and write four of their favorite idioms from their part of the book, one in each box on the top row of their paper.

6. Next, instruct students to create a funny illustration to go along with each idiom. Students should sketch these pictures in the boxes on the bottom row, directly below the corresponding idiom. At the end of the lesson, invite groups to share their idioms and to display their illustrations.

TWO-PART LESSON: SYMBOLISM

PART 1: DEFINING AND IDENTIFYING SYMBOLISM

Explanation

Symbols are everywhere we look, in visual, auditory, and verbal/written form. They can quickly convey concepts and ideas that would otherwise take many words to spell out—and, in many cases, would likely not be as effective. The more aware students become of the symbols in their everyday lives, the easier it will be for them to draw on the symbolism that various types of text have to offer. In this lesson, we deal simply with the nature of symbols and have students play a fun game to become familiar with them. In the following lesson, we delve into symbolism in literature.

Skill Focus

Applying knowledge of figurative language; creating mental images to aid comprehension; responding to texts through a variety of methods; explaining the effects of imagery; using symbols to express ideas

Materials & Resources

Text

- Any age-appropriate, primarily graphic text on symbols (Suggested for this lesson: *The Kids' Book of the 50 Great States*)

Other

- 3" x 5" index cards, approximately 20 per small group
- Pocket chart

Prior to the Lesson: Prepare a few symbol cards to prompt students to think of their own symbols. You can likely find excellent pictures on the Internet by using the "Images" feature on the Google toolbar. Some symbols you could make yourself or find on the Internet include: a square or rectangle with or without lettering showing the color green (environmental), restroom symbols for male and female, the wheelchair-access symbol, or a picture of a bald eagle.

STEPS

1. Write the word "Symbol" on the board. Ask students what the word means. Have them turn to a buddy and explain their understanding of the word. After students have shared, clarify for them a general definition of *symbol*: a sound or sign that represents something else.

2. Underneath the word "Symbol," write these categories: "verbal," "visual," "written." Explain that these are different types of symbols that are common in our everyday lives. Give examples of each, such as:

   Verbal/Auditory: These are sounds that represent an idea. When the school bell rings in the morning, for example, it means that school is ready to begin.

   Visual/Pictures: These symbols are seen, such as a red light at the corner or an electronic sign showing a figure walking at a pedestrian crossing. These don't involve written words.

   Written: These could range from musical notes to words on street signs. In fact, you might want to point out to students that letters themselves are symbols!

3. Discuss other symbols students may have seen, such as those encountered on family trips. Read from the preselected text, show any illustrations, and discuss some of the common symbols used. Ask students if they have seen these symbols and what information they convey or what emotions they inspire.

4. Set up small groups and give each group 10–20 index cards. Ask the groups to brainstorm as many symbols as they can within a 5- to 10-minute time frame. To get them started, distribute to each group a few of the cards you've prepared ahead of time (see Prior to the Lesson). Tell them to think of symbols at school, in sports, in government, in the workplace, and beyond. Have them depict only the symbol and not what it stands for.

5. Collect all the cards. Shuffle them, randomly divide them into equal sets, and redistribute them (with the symbol face down) to the groups. Have the first group expose their top card. Tell the class they have five seconds to identify what the symbol stands for. If no one in the group responds, the next group gets to respond, and so forth until some team earns the point. The goal is to earn the most points for correct responses.

PART 2: SYMBOLISM IN LITERATURE

Explanation

Whether they realize it or not, most students have already been exposed to a lot of symbolism in literature, most commonly through fairy tales and fables. In this lesson, students analyze a fable that relies upon an important symbol. Lessons on symbolism help young readers prepare for greater complexity in text.

Skill Focus

Applying knowledge of figurative language; creating mental images to aid comprehension; using graphic organizers; responding to texts through a variety of methods; explaining the effects of imagery; using symbols to express ideas

Materials & Resources

Text

- Narrative text with strong symbols (Used in this lesson: *The Lotus Seed* by Sherry Garland)

Other

- Chalkboard or transparency

- Colored chalk or overhead markers

Bonus Ideas

You can analyze any number of fairy tales and cartoons for their symbolism: white knights (goodness, chivalry), princesses (innocence, beauty), stepmothers (evil), fairy godmothers (goodness, power), apples (evil), and kings (power). Have students make a chart of symbols from their favorite fairy tales or cartoons and draw or write what they represent.

STEPS

1. Review the previous day's lesson on symbolism. Tell students that authors also use symbolism in their writing to help readers better understand their ideas. You might add that symbolism is considered a rather sophisticated special effect (though it *is* used early on in children's fairy tales). When symbolism is used in text, it causes the reader to think beyond the literal level of text. If readers aren't careful, they might miss the meaning altogether!

2. Read aloud the preselected text and ask students to listen for a symbol that represents an important idea in the story. For example, the sample text begins as a young girl in Vietnam sees the emperor cry on his loss of the throne. To remember him, she plucks a seed from a lotus pod in the imperial garden. Wrapped in a piece of silk, the seed offers her comfort for many years. As a civil war threatens her life, the girl, who has become a young widow with children, is forced to flee her homeland. She takes her treasure, the seed, with her to start a new life. Years later, her grandson finds the seed, plants it, and forgets where it is. The grandmother is greatly saddened by the disappearance of the seed. One day in spring, the grandmother discovers a flourishing lotus blossom—the flower of her native country.

3. After reading, draw the central symbol(s) on the board or a transparency. For the sample book, draw a lotus blossom with petals large enough to write in. Start the discussion by writing in one of the petals, "Her Country," and share that the blossom symbolized her native country of Vietnam. Ask what else the lotus represented. A list of possible responses follows:

   - memories of the crying emperor
   - downfall of her country
   - hardships she has endured
   - heritage/culture of her people
   - survival
   - loss of her husband

   Record students' responses on individual lotus petals.

4. Close by pointing out that symbols make us think and enjoy text on a different level. Ask students if they can think of important symbols from other fables or fairy tales.

Accessing Prior Knowledge

We now know that reading is an active process of meaning construction in which readers connect old knowledge with new information they encounter in the text (Harris and Hodges, 1995). If we envision this process as a formula, it would be: Old knowledge plus new knowledge equals comprehension. Thinking about it this way helps to highlight two important factors involved in teaching young readers. First, students often assume they have a one-way relationship with the printed page: It's there to tell them everything. An important part of the teacher's job is to help students realize they bring a great deal to the page. Rather than one-way, the relationship is always interactive. Second, because every reader brings a different, indeed unique, constellation of experiences and knowledge to the page, every reader is reading and comprehending uniquely.

The lessons in this section are primarily intended to help you develop the first factor—students' ability to call upon and make use of the background knowledge that they already have. Before saying a bit more about that, it's important to point out that frequently a teacher must go beyond helping students retrieve knowledge and must, in addition, actually help them build that knowledge. Many children, especially low achievers, have had limited experiences in their young lives. They have significant gaps in their exposure to text and world knowledge.

Good teachers are aware of this with every lesson they teach, realizing that a key part of their work is to help such students lay that all-important foundation. If the class is studying Egypt and some children have never left the boundaries of their community, a teacher needs to pull down the map, go to the Internet to do research, show them pictures, and engage them in discussions to give them experiences that will help to make them successful. Only when the reader can associate a text with memories and experiences does it become anchored in the reader's mind (Keene and Zimmermann, 1997). Staying mindful of this daily certainly takes effort on the teacher's part. But when comprehension is the reward, the payoff for both student and teacher is immense and worth all the effort.

Dramatizing the meaning of a word, as two girls do here for the word *accept*, is an excellent way for students to make connections.

You'll find that the lessons in this section use different ways to tap (and sometimes to build upon) students' prior knowledge. In one lesson, you'll ask students to retrieve what they know and add to it new information from text as they dynamically experience the meaning construction "formula" in action. In other lessons, you'll ask students to make different kinds of connections—text-to-self, text-to-text, and text-to-world—to deepen their understanding of what they're reading. Because building meaning vocabulary and concepts is a powerful means of developing background knowledge, one lesson focuses on how students can identify, research, and dramatize (for better recall and plain fun) unknown words. And, because you're working with students at upper grades who are capable

Students take notes as they put prior knowledge together with new information during reading.

of taking different points of view, another lesson engages students in using their prior knowledge to assume different roles in narrative text. There is even a lesson on analogies, which are a wonderful means of having students draw upon their own experiences to understand relationships among words. Doing this in isolation helps them focus on building thinking skills, and in context helps them develop both skills and content knowledge.

Let's take a look now at different ways you can prepare students to approach the printed page. Your goal is clear: to give them a better sense of how what they already know can help them come away from the page knowing even more.

NEW INFORMATION + PRIOR KNOWLEDGE: THE FORMULA

Explanation

This lesson calls attention to a simple "formula" that most students will find easy to grasp. When readers encounter new information and add it to their prior knowledge, they gain new knowledge. First through your modeling and then through direct experience, students learn the way this formula operates with real text.

Skill Focus

Using prior knowledge; using graphic organizers; making predictions about text; clarifying main ideas and details

Materials & Resources

Text

- Any grade-appropriate nonfiction text about which students have some background knowledge (Used in this lesson: *Year of the Ojibwa* by Sharman Apt Russell)

Other

- Blank transparency
- 1 index card for each student

STEPS

1. On the board or a transparency, draw a three-column chart. Title the columns "New Information," "Prior Knowledge," and "New Knowledge/ What I've Learned." Explain that good readers use new information along with prior knowledge to gain new knowledge. Tell students that they might envision it as a formula. Add a plus sign and an equal sign to your chart, as shown in the diagram below:

New Information +	Prior Knowledge =	New Knowledge/ What I've Learned

2. Now tell students that you are going to show them how you put the formula into action. Read aloud the first pages of your preselected text and demonstrate for students how you arrive at new learning. Fill in the appropriate chart columns as you read. Below is an example of a teacher's think-aloud, based on the sample text. For this text, which is about Ojibwa traditions, you'll read to figure out what the Ojibwa people think about these traditions.

Teacher's Read-Aloud	Teacher's Think-Aloud at Marked Places in Text
(1) It is the 1800s. A snowstorm is blowing hard outside your wigwam. You are a small boy and your father asks you to step out of your family's cozy home to "shoot the snow." (2) He puts a piece of birch bark on the end of a sharp arrow. Then he sets the birch bark on fire and fits the arrow to a bow. "Go outside," he urges you. "Hit the snow right in the eye." You step out of the wigwam as he watches. You shoot your arrow into the night, into the thickly falling snow. (3) Then you hurry back inside and go immediately to bed. Your mother promises that when you awake, the snowstorm will be gone. You fall asleep quickly, pleased and proud.	(1)"Since 'shoot the snow' is inside quotes, this must be the special tradition. I'll write 'shoot the snow' in the New Information column. Also, they start their tradition at an early age. I'll write this in New Information column." (2) "His father watches the small boy shoot the arrow into the thick snow. I'll write that in the New Information column. When I did something new, my dad always watched me to make sure I did it correctly. So I'll write that in the Prior Knowledge column." (3) "The boy goes to bed pleased and proud of what he did. I'll write this in the New Information column. I know when I'm proud of something, it must be important to me. I'll write this in the Prior Knowledge column."

3. You might draw conclusions about what you have learned like this:

Now let's look at the information in the first two columns. I have learned that the Ojibwa have a tradition of going out to "shoot the snow." They begin this at an early age. This tells me that it must be pretty important. The father watching is also very significant. The father must want to make sure the tradition is being carried out correctly. Finally, the boy is pleased and proud. This tells me that he feels good about completing this tradition. Now let's return to the focus of our reading, "What do the Ojibwa people think about traditions?" I can conclude that the Ojibwa cherish their traditions and think they are very important. I will write that in the third column.

New Information +	Prior Knowledge =	New Knowledge/ What I've Learned
(1) "shoot the snow" (1) start this tradition at an early age (2) father watches (3) boy is pleased and proud	(2) My dad watched me when I did something new. (3) When I am proud of something, it is important to me.	The Ojibwa people cherish their traditions and think they are very important.

4. Next, distribute a copy of the text and an index card to each student. Instruct them to make a blank chart like that in Step 1. Walk around to see that all students have charts set up correctly and are ready to go.

5. Pose a guiding question about the next section of the text. For example, for the sample book you might ask, "Why do you think sugar mapling is one of the family's most important traditions?" Direct students to read until they feel they have learned enough to answer the question. Instruct them to follow your model and fill in the first two columns on their index-card charts as they read. Once they feel they have learned enough to answer the question, they should fill in the third column.

6. Continue in this way until the students have completed the text selection or the portion of it that you've designated as today's reading. Invite students to share their charts and to explain why they've filled in each column as they have.

MAKING CONNECTIONS: TEXT-TO-SELF

77

Explanation

This is the first of a series of three lessons introducing the three basic kinds of connections that good readers make consistently before and during reading. This first lesson focuses on text-to-self connections, which involve readers' calling on their own prior knowledge and experience to help them make sense of text. Struggling readers seem to read right through the text without any interaction. Starting, quite literally, with a jolt, this lesson will help all students learn how to generate connections between their lives and their reading.

Skill Focus

Making connections between text and personal experience; using prior knowledge; coding text; making predictions about text; using repair strategies

Materials & Resources

Text

- Any grade-appropriate text about which you can make personal connections

- Multiple copies of a text about which students can make connections

Other

- 1.5-volt battery, two wires, and 1.5-volt lightbulb (you may be able to locate these items in your classroom science kit or around your house)

- Several sticky notes, all of one color, for each student

- 1 large piece of chart paper divided into 3 columns and titled: "Text-to-Self," "Text-to-Text," and "Text-to-World"

STEPS

1. Begin by presenting a simple science demonstration. Assemble the battery, wires, and lightbulb. Connect one end of a wire to the lightbulb and the other end to the positive (+) end of the battery. Then connect one end of the second wire to the lightbulb and the other end to the negative (–) end of the battery. When all of these are connected properly, they should form a complete circuit and the bulb should light up.

2. Now that, hopefully, students are intrigued, explain that the process you've just demonstrated illustrates what happens when we read. Good readers call on personal experiences, prior knowledge, opinions, and emotions and connect them to the information in the text. Each reader's unique connections cause a lightbulb to light up—the bulb of comprehension! These connections are called "text-to-self" connections.

3. Display the text you've selected for modeling. Read aloud, pausing at appropriate points to think aloud as you make personal connections with the text. Instead of saying, "I made a text-to-self connection," use authentic language. A sampling of introductory phrases that work well for these kinds of connections follows:

   - This reminds me of . . .

   - If that were me . . .

   - _____ has happened to me, too.

   - I felt like him/her when I . . .

4. Tell the class it's their turn. Distribute to each student the book you've selected for students' reading, along with several sticky notes. Instruct students to find several things in the text that remind them of something in their own lives. Once they've identified something, they should write the connection on a sticky note and place the note near the relevant text.

5. Call students' attention to the chart paper. Have students come forward to place all their sticky notes in the text-to-self section of the chart. Invite volunteers to read aloud some of their connections.

6. As students place and share their notes, guide them as necessary to make sure the connections are substantive and meaningful. For example, for a reading selection about a girl's strong bond with her dog, students who simply state, "I have a dog, too," could make a more meaningful connection if they noted the nature of their relationship with the dog. Naturally, you want to be sensitive here since these are personal connections. But it's important to help upper-grade students probe the connection as deeply as possible.

MAKING CONNECTIONS: TEXT-TO-TEXT

Explanation

This second lesson in a series of three introduces text-to-text connections. This type builds as the literary history of a reader grows: As readers encounter new texts, they construct increasingly deeper understanding by drawing on what they have learned from prior texts. Perhaps they're reminded of a character with similar traits, a comparable plot twist, or another story by the same author. Making these connections explicit, as students do here, enhances comprehension.

Skill Focus

Making connections among texts; using prior knowledge; coding text; making predictions about text; using repair strategies

Materials & Resources

Text

* A text about which you can easily make a connection with something else you've read

* Multiple copies of a text about which students can make these same kinds of connections

Other

* Several sticky notes, all of one color (but a different color from the previous lesson's notes), for each student

* Chart from the previous lesson

Bonus Ideas

Consider adding a flashlight to the classroom. During share time in the author's chair, during transition times, or at the end of the day, allow students to turn on the flashlight and shine it on the ceiling (only!) as they share aloud a connection they have made during reading.

STEPS

1. Review with students what they learned in the previous lesson—that good readers use personal experiences to make connections with texts. Explain that that's only one kind of possible connection. Sometimes readers may not personally have had an experience that helps them understand the text. They may, however, remember something similar from another text they've read. This kind of connection is called "text-to-text."

2. Display the text you've selected for modeling. Read aloud, pausing at appropriate points to think aloud as you draw connections with other texts you've read. Try to use authentic language. A sampling of sentences that work well for these kinds of connections follows:

   * This reminds me of the main character from [book title].

   * This reminds me of the setting in [book title].

   * This problem is similar to the problem in [book title].

   * The theme of this book is the same as [book title].

3. Tell the class it's their turn. Distribute to each student the book you've selected for students' reading, along with several sticky notes. Instruct students to find several things in the text that remind them of something they've read in another text. Once they've identified something, they should write the connection on a sticky note and place the note near the relevant text.

4. Call students' attention to the chart paper. Have students come forward to place all their sticky notes in the text-to-text section of the chart. Invite volunteers to read aloud some of their connections.

5. Conclude by pointing out the remaining blank column, titled "Text-to-World." Ask students if they can anticipate what this kind of connection might involve. Tell them they'll find out for sure in tomorrow's lesson.

MAKING CONNECTIONS: TEXT-TO-WORLD

Explanation

This final lesson in a series of three focuses on text-to-world connections. Readers bring not only their own personal and literary histories to their reading, they also bring their world knowledge. The more they know about historical and current events and happenings in science, the greater their world knowledge. Although this type of connection is often more difficult for students because they do not yet have extensive exposure to the greater world, teachers can help bridge the gap by modeling how to tap into what one does know and by providing opportunities for students to increase their awareness. This lesson suggests ways to do both.

Skill Focus

Making connections between text and personal experience or world events; using prior knowledge; coding text; making predictions about text; using repair strategies

Materials & Resources

Text

- Any grade-appropriate text about which you can easily make a connection with your world knowledge (Used in this lesson: *New York's Bravest* by Mary Pope Osborne)

- Multiple copies of a text about which students can make these same kinds of connections

Other

- Several sticky notes, all of one color (but a different color from the previous lessons' notes), for each student

- Chart from the two previous lessons

STEPS

1. Briefly review with students what they learned in the previous two lessons—that good readers use both personal experiences and their knowledge of other texts to make connections with what they're reading. Explain that there is a third kind of connection readers need to make. Sometimes readers need to think beyond their own personal lives and reading experiences to their knowledge of the larger world to better understand a text. We refer to this as making "text-to-world" connections.

2. Read aloud a selection that will be easy to connect with a familiar world event or world experiences. For example, the sample text is the story of Mose Humphreys, a dedicated and heroic firefighter in the 1840s. For this text, you might show how thinking about firefighters during 9/11 or recent fires that have been reported in your local news helps you better understand the important role Mose Humphreys must have played in his time.

3. Next, distribute to each student the book you've selected for students' reading, along with several sticky notes. Instruct students to find several things in the text that remind them of something they know about the outside world. Once they've identified something, they should write the connection on a sticky note and place the note near the relevant text. To guide students as they look for these kinds of connections, suggest that they pose questions like the following:

   - How does this remind me of the real world?
   - Has this problem happened in the real world?
   - Has something like this been reported in the news?
   - Have I seen something like this on TV?
   - Is this similar/different from an environmental issue in the real world?
   - Is this similar/different from a social issue in the real world?
   - Is this similar/different from a conflict in the real world?

4. Call students' attention to the chart paper. Have students come forward to place all their sticky notes in the text-to-world section of the chart. Invite volunteers to read aloud some of their connections.

5. You might follow up this lesson by giving each student six sticky notes—two of each color used in these three lessons. In a new text, have students try to locate two examples of each type of connection and use sticky notes color-coded the same way as in the lessons to mark different kinds of connections. (The use of all three connections in a text will be further explored in the next lesson.)

CONNECTIONS COME TOGETHER

Thus far, for instructional reasons, we have separated the three kinds of connections. But in this lesson, students learn that most texts offer a combination of connections—text-to-self, text-to-text, and text-to-world. First through your modeling, and next through their own direct experience, students will come to realize that almost all reading involves making all three kinds of connections.

Skill Focus

Making text-to-text connections; making connections between text and personal experience or world events; using prior knowledge to aid in comprehension of text; monitoring comprehension; coding text

Materials & Resources

Text

- Any grade-appropriate text about which all three kinds of connections can be made naturally (Used in this lesson: *The Memory Coat* by Elvira Woodruff)

- Additional text for making text-to-text connections (Used in this lesson: *Eyewitness: Russia* by Kathleen Berton Murrell)

- For each student: a copy of the same text used for modeling or a similar text

Other

- A sheet of unlined paper for each student and for the teacher

STEPS

1. Remind students that connections not only help readers comprehend as they read but they also help readers remember what they've read. Review briefly the three kinds of connections students have learned in the previous three lessons. Explain that good readers make all three connections automatically while they're reading. This lesson will illustrate how the three different kinds of connections can be made naturally during the reading of one text.

2. Hold up a sheet of unlined paper and demonstrate how you fold it in half lengthwise. Explain that you'll use this paper much like a double-entry journal (see lesson on p. 37) to record the connections that you can make with the text. Write "Connections" on the outside cover of the folded booklet. Then open the booklet and write "What the Text Is About" on the top left and "Connection/Type of Connection" on the top right.

3. Tell students that for this lesson you will be using codes to refer to the three types of connections. Text-to-self connections will be coded as *TS*; text-to-text as *TT*; and text-to-world as *TW*.

4. Display the preselected text. Begin to read it aloud, modeling how you make connections as you read. For example, for the sample text, you might pause on the first page after reading that the story begins "far away in Russia." You might mention that you have recently read an informational book called *Eyewitness: Russia*. Share something like the following:

   What I read about the history of Russia and its people in the informational book helps me understand this story a little better. I'm also recalling two things about Russia from that book that got my attention. One was that Russia spans eleven time zones—I thought that was amazing! Also, I loved reading about how the onion domes were constructed. If you've ever seen pictures of Russia, you've probably seen those beautiful domes.

5. Next, ask students, "What kind of connection have I just made?" When they respond, tell them that you're going to add that observation to your journal. Display the booklet and write "Takes place in Russia long ago" under "What the Text Is About." Under "Connection/Type of Connection," write "book—*Eyewitness: Russia/ TT*."

6. Continue reading. For the sample book, you might pause on page 4 after reading the description of how the house becomes filled with a large and lively extended family. Here you could share aloud something like the following:

   This reminds me of long ago when I was little and my family and my mother's brothers' and sisters' families gathered at my grandmother's house. What a commotion we all caused! I'll bet it was a lot like this!

- Connections depend upon a culture of reading. If your students have not had broad experiences with lots of books, read aloud to them and expose them to a good deal of self-selected reading time, ideally on a daily basis. If possible, set aside 30 minutes for your read-aloud and 20 minutes for students to read whatever they choose. Build your classroom library so that it includes several hundred books and other printed materials—magazines, how-to manuals, recipe books, driving manuals, pamphlets, and even take-out menus. It may seem like a daunting task. But building this culture of literacy is critically important and it will pay off for your students.

- To help students build background knowledge about real-world current events, consider holding regular class discussions on topics such as war, racism, natural disasters, patriotism, pollution, and global warming. A great resource is www.timeforkids.com.

- Set up three different boxes in the classroom library. Label each with the name of a type of connection, such as "Text-to-Self." Encourage students to use sticky notes to indicate connections they have made and then to place books in the boxes according to these connections. Many times students will be able to connect with the same events or ideas in books as their classmates.

7. In your booklet, under "What the Text Is About," write "house filled with family" and under "Connection/Type of Connection," write "my grandmother's house/*TS.* "

8. Continue reading aloud until you come to a natural text-to-world connection. In the sample book, the family immigrates to America through Ellis Island; explain you'll write this under "What the Text Is About." Then explain that you connect to this event based on your awareness of the importance of Ellis Island in U.S. history and/or on news accounts of people immigrating to the United States today to seek citizenship. Write one or both of these under "Connection/Type of Connection" and note *TW.*

9. Tell students it's their turn. Distribute a sheet of unlined paper to each student, along with a copy of the text students will be using for this lesson. Have them follow your model to create booklets and to use the booklets as they read. Circulate among students and guide them as needed to be sure that they are correctly coding their connections as *TS, TT,* or *TW.* If time permits, have students share their observations with the whole class.

DEVELOPING VOCABULARY THROUGH MEANINGFUL EXPERIENCES

Explanation

Broadening and deepening a reader's vocabulary provides more than word knowledge. It also enhances the background conceptual knowledge he or she has to call on during reading. This lesson invites students to identify difficult words and to explore them through dramatizing their meanings. This kind of active learning is a great way to improve memory, and it's a lot of fun at the same time!

Skill Focus

Making connections between text and personal experience or world events; using prior knowledge; coding text; making predictions; using repair strategies; using electronic resources for research; learning vocabulary through drama

Materials & Resources

Text

- Any grade-appropriate text with challenging words

- Multiple copies of this text for students

Other

- A set of VIP strips for each student

- 1 piece of lined paper for each group

- Computer access (Recommended site: www.allwords.com)

STEPS

1. Remind students of the importance of making connections during reading. Tell them that today's lesson will help them build both their background conceptual knowledge and their word knowledge. Knowing more words and more concepts will give them that much more to connect to while they're reading. They'll get to learn the words and concepts in a different way—by dramatizing them.

2. Distribute copies of the preselected text to students. Warn students ahead of time that this book contains quite a few challenging words. Read aloud until you come to a word that you are certain most students would not know.

3. Discuss with students what they do when they come to an unknown word like this one in their independent reading. Help them sort out what they should do if the word does not cause them to lose comprehension (continue reading) versus what should happen if they cannot understand the surrounding material without knowing the word (examine the word and try to figure out its meaning).

4. Hand out VIP strips and have students write a large question mark on each one ("?"). Now have students read several more text sections. When they encounter an unknown word that obstructs comprehension and context clues have not helped, they are to place a VIP strip directly under the word.

5. After reading, have students return to their VIP strips and read out the words. List these words on the board. Keep a tally of repeated words. Circle the words with the greatest number of tally marks.

6. Set up small groups. Assign several circled words to each group. Have students write their words on a piece of paper, then use a computer-based or standard dictionary to look up their words and find the definition that best fits how the word is used in the text. As well, provide computer access to each group and have them go to a recommended site to find the origins and etymology of their words. Have them write their findings next to the word on their piece of paper.

7. With all this information in hand, students are ready to generate and perform for the class a brief skit that illustrates the meaning of one or two of their words. For example, if the students located the word *haughty* in their text, their skit could go something like this: One student walks across the classroom in a normal fashion; another student walks in a slouching and grumpy manner; while a third student strides across the room with his/her nose in the air to indicate how sneeringly proud or haughty he or she is feeling. After this little performance, the students can offer a short explanation of the word.

LOOKING THROUGH DIFFERENT EYES

Explanation

This lesson challenges students to explore narrative text from unusual perspectives—either by taking on the persona of one of the story's characters or by looking at events through the eyes of an invented character. It thereby calls on students to analyze characters and events carefully, and at the same time to use their own life experiences to consider literature through different sets of eyes. Lessons like this help students develop greater ownership and interest in literature as they relate it to their own lives.

Skill Focus

Responding to texts through a variety of methods and through different perspectives; using prior knowledge; making connections between text and personal experience or world events

Materials & Resources

Text

- A narrative text that will capture students' attention (Used in this lesson: "The Necklace" by Guy de Maupassant)

Other

- Several index cards describing characters and scenarios (see Prior to the Lesson)
- 1 sheet of lined paper for each student
- 1 sheet of lined paper for each group

Prior to the Lesson: Either choose or create new characters central to the problem/dilemma in the story you've selected. For example, in "The Three Little Pigs," you might choose the wolf or you might create new characters such as a salesman for each pig's building materials or the pigs' uncle, who bargains with the wolf not to bother the pigs. On separate index cards, list these characters and hypothetical situations they've become involved in. Possible ideas for the sample story are presented at right.

> You are Mathilde Loisel's husband. You have been to a counselor to learn to say "no" to your wife. On a replay of the story, you now give her the invitation and listen to her response. What will you say to her this time?
>
> You are Dear Abby and you've received a letter from Mathilde after the ball asking what to do about the lost jewels. What do you advise?
>
> You are the wise sister of Mathilde. After losing the necklace, she has come to you for solutions to her problem. How will you advise her?
>
> You are a judge. Mathilde is furious that she has wasted years of her life. She sues her friend for the necklace she gave her long ago. How do you rule and why?

STEPS

1. Tell students that readers can gain a better grasp of a story's plot and characters if they look at the story through different eyes and assume a particular perspective. For instance, for "Cinderella," a reader might imagine that Cinderella is a classmate and friend. What would the student say and do if he/she suspected Cinderella was being mistreated by her family? (Perhaps speak to a guidance counselor or teacher.) Point out that in doing this, readers are calling on their prior knowledge as well as gaining new perspective on the narrative's characters.

2. Display the text. Distribute a sheet of paper to each student. Tell students that they should pay particular attention to the characters—to their traits, emotions, and actions—as you read and to take notes as they listen.

3. Read the story aloud and engage the class in a brief discussion about the characters and their traits. Now tell students that it's time for them to look at the story and the characters through different eyes.

4. Set up small groups. Distribute to each group a card describing a character and situation and a sheet of paper. Tell students they have 10–15 minutes to plan their responses. Instruct groups to use information as presented in the text unless their card advises them to do otherwise; outline on paper the main points the group will present; write their response in the first person from the point of view of the character described on the card; and choose a spokesperson to deliver the response that all group members have planned.

5. When the allotted time is up, invite each group to present their responses to the class. Engage the whole class in a brief discussion about each presentation. You might use questions such as the following to guide the discussion: Do you feel differently about one or more of the characters after this exercise? Do you like the story more or less after having done this exercise?

USING ANALOGIES TO DEEPEN UNDERSTANDING

Explanation

A study of analogies can seem like a dull and even useless exercise. However, not only does work with analogies prove helpful for test taking, it can also offer opportunities for critical thinking and analysis that improve the way a reader's mind operates. And analogies don't have to be irrelevant, abstract, or boring. As this lesson shows, they can deepen students' understanding of core content and concepts and can actually be fun!

Skill Focus

Using simple and complex analogies to aid comprehension; using prior knowledge; making connections between text and personal experience or world events

Materials & Resources

Text

- Any grade-appropriate informational text (Used in this lesson: a science chapter, "What Is an Electric Circuit?" from Harcourt Science, Grade 4)

Other

- 5 index cards for each partner set or small group

- 1 sheet of lined paper for each partner set or small group

STEPS

1. Start this lesson by writing a challenging riddle on the board:

    How are a football and a hamburger alike?

2. Organize students into small groups or partners and give each group/ partner a sheet of paper. Have them brainstorm and jot down how these two unlike items are similar. Tell them to come up with as many ideas as possible within the time limit. Allot about five minutes.

3. After students have brainstormed, ask them to share some of their findings. Their lists might include: both are made from animals, both can be held, both are brown, both are found at ball games, and so on.

4. List some of these ideas on the board and tell students that what they've done is to create an analogy: a comparison of the similarity between things that are dissimilar in other ways. Write the word *analogy* on the board.

5. Point out that analogies always involve a relationship between two or more items. For the analogy that a football is like a hamburger because they are both brown, the relationship is one of color. For the analogy that a football is like a hamburger because they can both be held, the relationship is one of size.

6. Present and discuss common analogous relationships. Write each on the board along with an example. (A few tips: Use a colon, the common convention for writing analogies, to depict the relationship. Rather than saying "is to" for the colon, use a full phrase to describe the relationship; this should prove much easier for and more meaningful to students. And remember, as recommended in the Explanation, to keep things simple at first, use only one pair—*kick : football*—rather than two pairs— *kick : football :: swing : bat*—as you present the categories and examples.) You might use a list like the following:

    - Function/purpose   kick : football ("Kick is what you do to a football.")
    - Part to whole   string : racket ("String is part of a racket.")
    - Worker and tool   player : baseball ("A player uses a baseball.")
    - Synonyms   begin : start ("Begin is the same as start.")
    - Antonyms   begin : end ("Begin is the opposite of end.")
    - Cause and effect   rain : flooding ("Rain causes flooding.")
    - Effect and cause   hunger : not eating ("Hunger is the result of not eating.")
    - Symbol and what it stands for   Statue of Liberty: freedom ("The Statue of Liberty stands for freedom.")

7. Now, use the model text to show students how familiarity with analogous relationships can deepen their understanding of what they're reading. For example, with the sample text, you might pair key topic words with potentially related words and challenge students to use creative thinking to come up with possible relationships. A list of examples, with possible relationships, follows:

   battery : pedal (Both transfer energy—one gives motion to a whole wheel and the other moves energy through a circuit.)

   circuit : path (A circuit *is* a path of electrical charges.)

   conductor : blanket (They have opposite functions. A blanket is an insulator.)

8. As another means of challenging students to use analogies to deepen reading comprehension, present sample key word pairs. Have students deduce the categories that describe the relationship between the two key words. Below are examples based on the sample text:

   conductor : insulator (opposites: one allows current to pass and one does not)

   battery : cell (same: a battery is an electric cell)

   current: light (cause/effect: electric current can cause illumination)

9. Next, distribute five index cards to each partner set or small group. Working with an assigned content textbook section, students should cull out keywords and use the words to write an analogy on one side of each card. On the back of each card, they should explain the relationship reflected by that card's analogy.

10. Finally, instruct students to exchange their cards. The partners/groups receiving the cards are to study only the front sides of the cards, to guess the analogy relationships, and then to check them with the back sides. Ask groups to set aside any cards they want to challenge. As a class, discuss and resolve any challenged cards.

Summarizing

Summarizing is a far more sophisticated task than it first might appear to experienced readers. All too often, summarizing is confused with merely choosing what is most important in text, but genuine summarizing goes far beyond that simple activity (Dole, Duffy, Roehler, and Pearson, 1991). The summarizing process actually calls on a number of higher-level thinking skills. To be able to create a summary, you must "discern the most central and important ideas in the text…generalize from examples or from things that are repeated…and ignore irrelevant details" (NRPR; NICHHD, 2000). The reader must not only separate what is most important from what is of lesser importance but must also synthesize the prioritized information to form a new text, of sorts, that stands for the original text. And we're asking all this of a child!

However, if we do it appropriately by setting a foundation and then slowly introducing the concept, teaching our young readers about summarizing is not only possible—it's definitely worth the effort. In fact, for a number of reasons, summarizing improves overall comprehension of text (Pearson and Duke, 2002). For example, summarizing can improve memory for what is read, both in terms of free recall and answering questions (NRPR; NICHHD, 2000).

With the distinct benefits of teaching children to summarize in mind, we must also understand what research says is necessary for this learning to take place. Many, if not most, children require direct instruction in the different skills and sub-tasks involved in summarizing. The teacher's role is critical in explaining what must occur and in modeling how the process looks and sounds. Further, to produce good oral and written summaries of text, students must have adequate time for applying what they've learned and for practicing summarizing. With instruction and practice, not only will they become better at summarizing, they'll become better readers (Pearson and Duke, 2002).

This cereal box book report includes a summary of the book—much like a blurb on a published book.

As you'll see from the range of lessons in this section, summarization can take many different forms, using both fiction and nonfiction pieces. Students in these upper grades need to learn to sort between what's interesting and what's important in text, a crucial skill to being able to derive the essence of the text. They'll learn to deduce both the topic sentences and main idea of a piece using context clues; summarize plot by investigating, through acting out scenarios, the basic construction of a piece (beginning, middle, end) and its core elements; and differentiate between vital points and interesting details by coming up with a summary of one all-important invention: potato chips! Students will practice taking notes by analyzing want ads; deconstruct the idea of theme via a look at common

Taking good notes is an important step toward effectively summarizing a text.

holidays; and actually have fun with the oft-dreaded task of outlining by creating a life-size chart. Finally, they'll learn how to group (categorize/classify) and prioritize information and concepts.

Capturing the essence of a reading selection . . . this is what summarizing is all about. Simple on the surface, yet quite a sophisticated task after all!

TOPIC SENTENCES: WHAT'S MISSING?

Explanation

Identifying the topic or gist of a paragraph, article, or passage is a sophisticated task. It is therefore a skill that needs to be taught, modeled, and practiced many times in many ways over the years. It is also a key step in the process of summarizing a piece of text. This lesson challenges students to make informed guesses about an article's topic and main ideas. It lends itself to use in both content areas and reading lessons.

Skill Focus

Summarizing main ideas and details in text; identifying topic sentences; clarifying main ideas and details; using text features; reading and navigating media text; making predictions about text

Materials & Resources

Text

- Multiple copies of newspaper article or other informational piece, prepared as described in Prior to the Lesson

- Book or other text that can aid in direct teaching of main idea concept (Recommended: *The Important Book* by Margaret Wise Brown; although simplistic, it is a very effective means of teaching main idea)

Other

- Sentence strips, one set for each pair/small group

- Sticky notes, one for each pair/ small group

- Paper clips

Prior to the Lesson: Find a newspaper article or informational piece in which the main idea comes across clearly. Make a photocopy (retaining original), then use a marker to black out the article's title and the main idea of each paragraph. Type each main idea on a sheet, make five or six photocopies of the sheet, and cut the sheets into sentence strips.

STEPS

1. Tell students that today's lesson focuses on main idea and supporting details and looks ahead to summarizing. Review the concept of topic sentence. Remind students that the title of an article or text selection often captures the main idea, or topic, of the entire piece and that each paragraph typically includes its own topic sentence. Identifying the overall topic, as well as the individual main ideas, are key steps toward summarizing a text. If you are using a book or other text to further illustrate the concept of main idea, read it aloud. For the recommended book, guide students to realize that the importance of each object described in the book is similar to the importance of a main idea in a paragraph.

2. Now set up partners or small groups. Distribute a copy of the prepared article to each pair or group. Explain that you have blacked out the title of the article and the main idea of each paragraph. Instruct partners/groups to preview the article by reading the first and last paragraphs. They should make predictions about the topic sentence of each paragraph.

3. Next, hand out to each pair or group a set of sentence strips. Have students read the article to figure out where each strip belongs. Instruct them to paper-clip each strip to the appropriate paragraph and to underline the supporting details in the paragraph.

4. Now read aloud the article one paragraph at a time. Call on volunteers to identify the main idea and the supporting details for each paragraph. Work with students as necessary to ensure that the elements of each paragraph are correctly identified before you move on to a subsequent paragraph.

5. When you've completed the article, distribute a sticky note to each pair or group. Have students jot down their best guess at a title for the entire article. Collect the sticky notes, and then reveal the title to see which pair/ group came closest to the original.

SUMMARIZING THE PLOT

Explanation

In order to effectively summarize a piece of fiction, it's important to analyze its basic construction—beginning, middle, and end. It's also important to examine its core elements—character, setting, plot, problem, and solution. In this lesson, students work with summarizing plot in two quite different ways—first by dramatizing and then by using a graphic organizer.

Skill Focus

Summarizing main ideas and details; identifying main events in a story's plot; using a graphic organizer; monitoring comprehension by coding text; responding to text through a variety of methods

Materials & Resources

Text

- Multiple copies of a grade-appropriate narrative text with a distinct plot and clear story elements

Other

- Several scenarios with clear plotline and story elements (see Prior to the Lesson)

- A set of 5 VIP strips for each small group

- 1 sheet of unlined paper for each small group

Prior to the Lesson: Jot down several short scenarios with a simple plotline and clear story elements for students to act out. One example follows:

- *beginning: main character (bicyclist) introduced and setting (country road) established*

- *middle: rising action—bicyclist hops on his bike and rides down the road*

- *middle: climax—a flat tire occurs*

- *middle: resolution—friend comes along with air pump and fills tire*

- *end/conclusion: friends shake hands, person hops back on the bike and rides away*

STEPS

1. Discuss with the class the typical text structure used for virtually all narratives—quite simply, stories are usually told in a format of what happens in the beginning, what happens in the middle, and then what happens at the end. Folded within each of these segments are the story elements of character, setting, plot, problem, and solution. Tell students that the best way to summarize a narrative is to first analyze its structure. Today they'll get to do that in two very different ways—by dramatizing and by mapping out a graphic organizer.

2. Set up small groups. Distribute a different scenario to each group. Have groups meet to discuss how they will perform it, to create a brief script for each part, and to decide on a director, actors, and set designer. (To keep things simple, the "set designer" might simply describe the setting, rather than design it.)

3. Invite each group forward to perform their scenario for the class. After each performance, have students discuss the story elements and explain why they decided to represent them as they did.

4. On the board or a transparency, draw a triangle-shaped diagram. Label it to represent both plot structure and story elements. Relate these components to the scenarios students have just acted out. See example diagram on page 90 at the end of the lesson.

5. Next, distribute a sheet of paper to each small group. Instruct students to draw a triangle in the center of the paper. Have them label the triangle to match the one on the board or transparency.

Bonus Ideas

For your student performances, consider using your overhead projector as a spotlight. Arrange for performing groups to stand in a just-right position so that the light from the projector forms a spotlight. Allow the groups about five–seven minutes to practice. Suggest that students grab props from around the room to add a little excitement to their performance. Let your students shine under the spotlight!

6. Distribute the preselected text to each small group, along with a sticky note cut into five VIP strips. Have students read the text. When they encounter a targeted plot segment/story element (for example, "beginning/setting"), they should write the information on a VIP strip and place it at the appropriate spot in the story. Circulate among groups to check their work.

7. Finally, have students remove the VIP strips from the text and place them in the correct positions on the triangle. They should wind up with a visual representation of the story's elements and plot events.

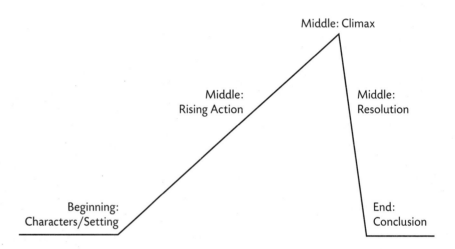

Middle: Climax

Middle:
Rising Action

Middle:
Resolution

Beginning:
Characters/Setting

End:
Conclusion

TWO-PART LESSON: IDENTIFYING WHAT'S WHAT

PART 1: DETERMINING WHAT'S MOST IMPORTANT

Explanation

This two-part lesson series gives students practice in a set of skills that they'll need at all grade levels, and even in college. In this first lesson, they'll first engage in a class discussion to help you create a classroom chart of guidelines for highlighting important ideas. They'll also put these guidelines into action to identify what's most important in a text and highlight it—the initial step in a methodical process that will lead to their creating a successful summary.

Skill Focus

Summarizing main ideas, events, and themes in texts; recalling significant details in text; categorizing and classifying ideas

Materials & Resources

Text

- A brief, grade-appropriate informational text (Used in this lesson: original article based on information about the invention of potato chips from www. enchantedlearning.com)

- A consumable, grade-appropriate magazine or newspaper for each partner set

Other

- A transparency of the selected text

- 2 highlighters in different colors for each partner set

- 1 sheet of chart paper

STEPS

1. Discuss with students the basic elements of a summary. Define a summary as "a short way of telling the most important points in a text." A good summary includes the main idea and supporting details. Tell students that in this two-part lesson they will have the opportunity to summarize material from a detailed, descriptive essay. Their job in this first lesson will be to highlight what is most important—the main idea—in a text. You might let them know that the skill they learn today they will need even in college. (That should impress them!)

2. Mount a piece of blank chart paper. List guidelines for the process good readers follow to highlight a text's key ideas. (This chart can be displayed permanently in your classroom for students' ongoing reference.) An example follows:

Guidelines for Highlighting the Most Important Ideas

1. Read the beginning and ending and look for an idea that is stated and later restated.

2. Look for key words that are often repeated.

3. Check to see if the big ideas are supported by interesting details, but don't confuse those interesting details with what's most important!

4. Never highlight more than half of the text.

5. Never highlight whole sentences—just words and phrases.

---

3. Be sure to encourage students' participation and discussion as you create the chart. Following are some things to point out to students during the class discussion:

- Beginning and ending sentences are not necessarily topic sentences. In fact, often in well-written nonfiction, authors use "hooks" to grab attention before revealing the topic.

- Main ideas aren't always spelled out explicitly as discrete topic sentences, especially in more sophisticated text.

- Editors and publishers may use "eye signals"—for example, italics, underlining, highlighting, or marginal definitions—to draw attention to certain important words. In some texts, these words aren't necessarily critical to constructing the main idea but have been called out for other illustrative reasons.

- What's interesting sometimes grabs a reader's attention more quickly than what's important and may therefore throw readers off track. (This is the focus of Part 2 of this lesson.)

- The above point is usually true of half a paragraph as well. That is, if half a paragraph has been highlighted, many details will assuredly be revealed already.

- There are lots of articles—*a*, *an*, *the*, and so on—in any writing selection but sheer quantity doesn't make them important.

4. Display the transparency of the preselected text passage. Read the whole passage aloud one time, and then return to the beginning. Read each sentence and model how you decide whether that statement is important enough to highlight. Think aloud as you make your decisions. The sample text, with highlighting and think-aloud comments, is shown on the following page.

Fussy Customer Leads to Invention

We've probably all been in uncomfortable situations when customers have complained about food in a restaurant. We can thank one of these disgruntled customers, however, for the invention of one of our nation's favorite snack foods—the potato chip! In 1853, George Crum, a chef at the Moon Lake Lodge in Saratoga Springs, New York, did not seem to be able to please a customer who ordered one of the restaurant's specialties—French fries. After receiving a second protest that the fries were too thick, Crum decided to annoy the customer by making the fries far too thin for the same complaint to be possible. Upon being served the thin fries, the customer was instead quite pleased by the new shape and thickness of the fry. And so the potato chip was born—all due to a customer's complaints!

"*Fussy, complained,* and *disgruntled* all have similar meanings. Because the meaning is the same and repeated several times, I'm thinking I need to highlight at least one of these adjectives. And they're all used to describe a customer, so that seems important, too."

"Because this is about an invention and because the potato chip is the invention, I'm sure those words should be highlighted."

"I think it's interesting to know when and where potato chips were invented and by whom."

"Wow! The potato chip was actually a modified French fry! That's pretty amazing, but it doesn't seem like the main point."

"I think it's funny that the potato chip was invented because this chef wanted to annoy someone. That's really interesting, but I don't think this is the main reason the author wrote this piece!"

"It's cool that the customer was pleased instead of annoyed!"

"This last idea sounds very much like the part I highlighted. It seems to be stressing it again. I think I've highlighted the right part."

5. At this point, you might summarize your key words into a main idea. For the sample, you might say, "I think this article is mainly about a disgruntled customer who led to the invention of the potato chip."

6. Set up partners. Distribute a magazine or newspaper and two different-colored highlighters to each pair. Have students select an article and use one highlighter to mark what they think are the important points as they go through the text the first time. Then, have them indicate final decisions (focusing on highlighting the fewest words possible) with the other color. (Be sure to retain students' articles to use in Part 2.)

TWO-PART LESSON: IDENTIFYING WHAT'S WHAT

PART 2: SORTING OUT AND SUMMARIZING

Explanation

This lesson, the second in a two-part series, helps students prioritize text information and then write a summary based on that information. They have already identified the main idea in a piece. Now they search for the supporting details, which are often more intriguing than the key point. Therefore, this lesson also encourages students to differentiate between what is merely interesting and what is centrally important in text.

Skill Focus

Summarizing main ideas, events, and themes in texts; recalling significant details in text; categorizing and classifying ideas

Materials & Resources

Text

- The text used in Part 1 of this lesson

- Partners' highlighted articles from Part 1

Other

- The highlighted text transparency from Part 1

- Blank transparency or chart paper

STEPS

1. Tell students that today they will continue looking at the same text but this time they will focus on ideas that are less significant than those highlighted in Part 1. Only after they are able to identify both the key point(s) and the supporting details in a text will they be ready to summarize it. Warn students that these kinds of facts are sometimes so fascinating that they distract readers. Many readers remember these interesting tidbits and ignore the big picture or the main idea. Good readers always identify both the main idea and the details and always know the difference.

2. Display the text transparency. Read back through the article and underline the parts that offer details about the main idea you've already identified. An example of the sample text, with appropriate details underlined, follows:

Fussy Customer Leads to Invention

We've probably all been in uncomfortable situations when customers have complained about food in a restaurant. We can thank one of these disgruntled customers, however, for the invention of one of our nation's favorite snack foods—the potato chip! In 1853, George Crum, a chef at the Moon Lake Lodge in Saratoga Springs, New York, did not seem to be able to please a customer who ordered one of the restaurant's specialties—French fries. After receiving a second protest that the fries were too thick, Crum decided to annoy the customer by making the fries far too thin for the same complaint to be possible. Upon being served the thin fries, the customer was instead quite pleased by the new shape and thickness of the fry. And so the potato chip was born—all due to a customer's complaints!

---

3. Next, using a new transparency or chart paper, create a simple T-chart to compare your findings and to illustrate the difference between what is simply interesting and what is most important in a text selection. As you record supporting information, make the point that these interesting details all support the main idea. You might say something like, "Notice that if an idea isn't connected to the main idea, I'm not listing it. The details I've chosen to include all add interesting facts about how the invention of the potato chip occurred." The example on page 95 is based on the sample text.

What's Interesting (supporting details)	What's Important (main idea)
1853	
George Crum, chef	
New York restaurant	A disgruntled customer led to the invention of the potato chip.
Making French fries	
Crum intended to annoy customer	
Customer loved it!	

Bonus Ideas

- To offer students further practice for summarizing topics and main ideas, cut out newspaper articles and remove the heading from each article. Have students read the articles and write their own headings. Then let them compare their version with the original heading to see if they managed to capture the essence that a professional writer had decided upon.

- Compare the statement of main idea and this summarized version of the text to show how this version is more detailed. Let students know that this elaborated version is often needed. To further illustrate this difference, supply students with book ads, blurbs, or reviews from publishing companies or from the Internet such as amazon.com and barnesandnoble.com. These sources often provide a one-line summary along with more detailed book descriptions. Have students study these and then try writing both a summarized and an elaborated version for some of their favorite books.

4. Continue discussing the chart by asking students if they would find the reading as appealing without the details. Hopefully, they'll agree that the details keep our attention. However, we just have to be sure to see the main idea through the interesting details.

5. Now, tell students that because you have determined both the main idea and the supporting details, you already have everything you need to write an effective summary. All you need to do is pull it back together. Model how you include both the main idea (although not necessarily as a first sentence) and supporting details. Point out how you purposely condense the material and how you present it as concisely as possible. A summary is not the time for creative flourishes or elaboration! An example summary for the sample text follows:

In 1853, George Crum, a New York chef, tried to annoy a customer who complained that the chef's French fries were too thick. He purposely created thin fries. But the customer enjoyed them. And that's how a disgruntled customer led to the invention of the potato chip.

6. Re-form the partner groups that worked together on Part 1. Hand back their highlighted magazine or newspaper articles and have them follow your model to underline supporting details and then to write summaries based on the information they have identified. When all have finished, invite partners to share their summaries with the whole class.

THINKING EFFICIENTLY: NOTE TAKING

Prior to the Lesson: *If you are not using the wordy ad provided in Step 4, you'll need to create your own example.*

STEPS

1. Explain to students that note taking is a lifelong skill, not only needed in school and college but also in the workplace as well as at home. Like summarizing, note taking requires a reader or listener to think about the essential meaning of something. Good note taking involves sorting out extraneous matter and recording only what's critical to remember and comprehend. Good note takers are also efficient. If they're listening to a lecture or a speech, they know they will lose the train of thought if they try to write down every little thing. If they're reading, they realize that copying out everything on a page isn't going to help them focus in on what's worth remembering. In life situations, too, note taking can be very handy. For example, if the phone rings at home and the caller wants to leave a message, it's far better to jot down a few notes rather than try to record every word.

2. Tell students that there are quite a few guidelines that can help them become good note takers. Today's lesson will focus on four of them. Write the following on a piece of chart paper:

Guidelines for Taking Notes

- Use abbreviations.
- Include important words.
- Write the fewest words possible.
- Make sense.

3. Display the newspaper ad transparency. Point out that classified ads provide an extreme example of condensed writing. Ads are typically billed according to length. The more you can say in the least amount of space, the better off you are! Advertisers, therefore, strive to meet all four of the criteria listed above. Read aloud and analyze the sample ad(s). You may need to help students interpret common abbreviations—for example, LR, FP, 3BR, W/D for a real estate ad.

4. Next, display the other transparency and distribute a sheet of paper to each student. Tell the class that this wordy ad has not yet been pruned. It would cost the advertiser quite a bit of money! Tell students that their challenge is to pare it down, using the fewest possible letters (not just words) that can be understood. You might want to establish a billing scale to see who can place the cheapest ad. (Ads are usually priced by the line, but unless

Explanation

Effective note taking and summarizing are related skills: They both require the listener/reader to extract the essence of a piece, to condense it, and to rephrase it succinctly. This lesson introduces students to the note-taking process through a fun "real-life" activity that focuses on several key subskills. In the next lesson, students will take off from this initial experience to engage in the full note-taking process.

Skill Focus

Summarizing main ideas, events, and themes in texts; clarifying main ideas and details; recalling significant details in text; skimming and scanning for information; taking notes

Materials & Resources

Text

- 2 or 3 newspaper classified ad(s) for goods, services, or real estate
- Wordy ad text (see Prior to the Lesson) that has not yet been pruned or edited

Other

- Transparency of the newspaper ads
- Transparency of the wordy ad text
- Chart paper

- Just as you encourage students to prune the classified ad in this lesson—assigning a billing scale that rewards the most tightly worded ad—you might assign a dollar amount to notes students take from their regular text reading to motivate them to be as concise as possible.

- Point out to students that text messaging involves another common use of abbreviations. Although many of those abbreviations would not be appropriate or acceptable for use in a newspaper ad, students may find them helpful in their own personal note taking. Invite students to share some of their favorite text messaging abbreviations.

- Create a center to help students practice note-taking skills through a practical application. On a tape recorder, record a number of phone messages of various lengths and complexities. Place the recorder on a table along with a small notebook (or special phone message tablets) and pencils. Invite students to take notes as they listen to the messages. Have students exchange and compare their notes to be sure that all necessary information has been recorded.

your students are using computers to write theirs, you might have to charge by the number of letters used.) Following is a sample wordy ad (and an efficiently worded version) you might use, or you can come up with your own:

I want you to rent my apartment that has three bedrooms and two bathrooms. You'll like the kitchen that has all of the major appliances (dishwasher, refrigerator, stove) included. If you've always wanted a fireplace, you're in luck! This apartment has a wood-burning fireplace. Also, the very large yard is fenced in. What a great feature this will be for you if you have a dog or if you have children. You can call me anytime at 902-555-4433.

Rent: 3BR, 2B, DW, ref., stove, FP, lg. fenced yd. Call 902-555-4433.

5. When students have finished rewriting the ad, call on volunteers who believe they have created cheap (but comprehensible) ads. Have them come forward to share these ads and invite class discussion.

Taking Notes From Informational Text

STEPS

1. Review with students what they learned about note taking in the previous lesson: Taking notes is an efficient process that allows the reader or speaker to pare down information and to record only what's critical to remember and comprehend. Tell students that in this lesson they will learn four additional guidelines for note taking. Display the chart you started in the previous lesson and list the additional guidelines. Discuss each guideline as you write it. The full list is above.

Guidelines for Taking Notes
• Use abbreviations.
• Include important words.
• Write the fewest words possible.
• Make sense.
• Capture the main idea.
• Use abbreviated headings/subheadings to organize.
• Indent to show levels of importance.
• Use bullets and/or numbers to sort and organize.

2. Display the transparency of the text. Read the text aloud, think aloud as you make decisions about what notes to record, and model how you take notes. A completed example for the sample text, with modeled notes, follows:

Sample Text	Notes
What is Sleep? When we sleep, we are in a state of being unconscious of our surroundings. There is a difference between being in a coma, though, and being asleep because we can be awakened by any strong stimulus like a loud noise, a light, or by movement. **Do All Living Things Sleep?** Higher vertebrates like mammals, birds and reptiles go into a state of being unconscious of their surroundings. Fish and amphibians reduce their awareness but do not sleep as higher vertebrates. Insects do not appear to sleep but do become inactive at times. **What Happens When the Body Doesn't Get Sleep?** After one full day without sleep, a person generally appears sluggish and irritable. For some people, however, just the opposite occurs—they are excitable because of adrenalin. After two days, concentration is extremely difficult. After three days of wakefulness, a person is likely to hallucinate and lose touch with reality.	Sleep? • Unconscious of surroundings • Not coma b/c can be awakened All Things Sleep? • Higher vertebrates do • Fish & amphib. reduce awareness • Insects inactive No Sleep? • 1 Day – sluggish, irritable or hyper • 2 Days – concentration difficult • 3 Days - hallucinate

3. Distribute a photocopied version of the other article, formatted like the model, to each student. Instruct students to follow the process you modeled: Read the text in the left-hand column and take notes in the right-hand column. Circulate among students to offer guidance as needed.

WHAT'S THE MESSAGE?

1. Tell students that today's lesson focuses on themes. Explain that a theme is an underlying message or meaning. Many books and stories have themes, but themes occur elsewhere as well. Before discussing literary themes, the class will have a chance to think about them in a different context—holidays and celebrations.

2. On the board list several holidays/celebrations. (Choose nonreligious holidays to avoid excluding or making uncomfortable any of the students.) Have the students vote to select one and then brainstorm what they usually do on that day. For example, if students choose Thanksgiving, they might mention such activities as baking a turkey or watching a parade. Help students realize that these activities are like "props" that support the underlying theme of the day. We need to go beyond the activities to ask: Why do we have a feast? Why are we getting together? What does the parade represent? Guide students to see that in one way or another all these activities reflect the underlying theme of gratitude.

3. Now relate the discussion to literature. Explain that an author expresses an underlying theme or message through a story's events, images, and characters. Very different stories, with very different plots, settings, and characters, may convey the same theme. Common literary themes include friendship, freedom, poverty, wealth, courage, bravery, responsibility, love, and peace.

4. Display the preselected book. Read aloud a chapter. Use chart paper to list key events. For the sample book, you might list:
   - encounter with Nazi soldiers on the street
   - shelters a Jewish friend from the Nazis
   - German soldiers arrive at door
   - Annemarie hides necklace from the soldiers, leaving imprint on her hand

5. Work with the class to extrapolate a theme from these actions and events. For the sample book, you might guide them by asking them to consider this question: What quality did Annemarie show during all these events? The answer could be expressed as one word, bravery or courage, or perhaps as a phrase: bravery or courage in standing up for one's beliefs.

6. Set up partners. Distribute a copy of the text and a set of VIP strips to each pair. Direct students to read to a certain point in the text. They are to place VIP strips at every point at which they believe the theme is conveyed through characters, actions, or images. Afterward, invite students to share their findings with the class.

Explanation

Recognizing and understanding a book's theme, or underlying message, is yet another way for a reader to distill or summarize the main point in a story. This lesson begins by having students extrapolate a theme from real-life holiday activities and then engages them in doing the same with a piece of literature.

Skill Focus

Identifying and analyzing themes; paraphrasing and summarizing using themes; coding text; identifying plot events; analyzing author's purpose

Materials & Resources

Text
- Any grade-appropriate narrative that clearly conveys a theme (Used in this lesson: *Number the Stars* by Lois Lowry)
- Multiple copies of this text for students

Other
- For each partner set: 2–3 sticky notes cut into VIP strips
- Chart paper

Bonus Ideas

- Challenge students to find a text quote that expresses the text's theme. Have them illustrate the quote. You might assemble these to create a class book or a bulletin board.

- Suggest that students having trouble discerning a story's theme use this sentence stem to get the process underway: "After I've read this (book, poem, essay), the author wants me to understand…"

OUTLINING

Explanation

Creating a successful outline requires students to sort and classify text points and to phrase these points concisely. Thus, outlining utilizes many of the same skills involved in summarizing. This lesson not only teaches students how to outline and to differentiate among topic, subtopics, and details, but it engages them kinesthetically in the process. Outlining is not usually this active, nor this much fun!

Skill Focus

Creating an outline to summarize; paraphrasing and summarizing using main ideas, events, details, and themes; clarifying main ideas and details; classifying and categorizing ideas; rereading to find details

Materials & Resources

Text

* Any grade-appropriate text that lends itself to outlining (Used in this lesson: Chapter 8 of *Holes* by Louis Sachar)

Other

* Sentence strips

* Tape, chart paper

* Sheet of notebook paper for each student

Prior to the Lesson: Create a sentence strip for each outline element (topic, subtopics, details) for the text you're using. For the sample text, the sentence strips are as follows: I. Yellow-Spotted Lizard; A. Description; 1. Eleven yellow spots; 2. Yellow-green body; 3. Six to ten inches long; 4. Yellow eyes; 5. Skin around eyes red; 6. Black teeth; 7. Milky-white tongue; B. Possible Names; 1. "Red-eyed" lizard; 2. "Black-toothed" lizard; 3. "White-tongued" lizard; C. Habitat; 1. Predatory birds; 2. Up to 20 lizards live together; 3. Deep holes; D. Food; 1. Small animals; 2. Insects; 3. Certain cactus thorns; 4. Shells of sunflower seeds

STEPS

1. Remind students that an outline expresses relationships among ideas by showing how the most important idea, or topic, relates to the lesser and then the least important ideas. Tell students this is called a hierarchical order. Explain that in today's lesson the whole class is going to work together to develop an outline for a particular text.

2. Read aloud or have students read individually the preselected text.

3. Distribute a sentence strip to each student. Write these three words on the board: *topic, subtopic, details*. Briefly discuss the meaning of each. Tell students that their sentence strip states a word or phrase from the text that is either a topic, a subtopic, or a detail.

4. Mount the chart paper; draw a left margin. Begin the outline by writing the title of the outline, "Chapter 8," in the center of the paper. Direct students to do the same on their notebook paper. (Note that—due to the way this particular book is set up—the outline title is simply the chapter number and does not provide any information about the topic.)

5. Next, ask students to identify the chapter's topic. They should be able to recognize that the entire chapter is about yellow-spotted lizards. Have the student with the sentence strip "I. Yellow-Spotted Lizard" come up to the chart. Discuss the use of Roman numerals in an outline, explaining they are used to indicate main topics. Have the student tape his/her sentence strip next to the margin. Instruct students to write this main topic on the left margin of their paper.

6. Explain that the next step in creating an outline is identifying a subtopic. Have students reread to decide upon a key idea that relates directly to the main topic. In the sample book, the third and fourth paragraphs reveal a detailed description of the yellow-spotted lizard. Announce that the student with the sentence strip "A. Description" should come forward. Discuss the use of uppercase letters in an outline, explaining they are used to indicate subtopics. Help the student to position the strip, with one indent, directly under the topic. Explain to students that the subtopic

describes the topic, and subtopics are indented once. Have students write the name of the subtopic on their paper, being sure to indent.

7. Ask if students know what comes next. Tell them they may look back at the book at this point. Together, identify "details" as the next element in the outline. Discuss the use of numbers in an outline, explaining they are used to indicate details. One at a time, invite students with sentence strips relating to "Description" to come forward and to tape their sentence strip correctly (i.e., with two indents) on the chart paper. Have students write these on their paper, being sure to indent twice.

8. Check to see whether students can guess what comes next. Help students, as needed, to realize that they now need to list a new subtopic. For the sample book, the student with the sentence strip "B. Possible Names" should come forward. Review correct outline formatting and have the student tape it in the correct spot on the chart. Have students write the name of this second subtopic on their paper, being sure to indent one space.

9. Continue this process until all sentence strips have been correctly positioned. A completed outline for the sample text follows:

Chapter Eight

I. Yellow-Spotted Lizard
  A. Description
    1. Eleven yellow spots
    2. Yellow-green body
    3. Six to ten inches long
    4. Yellow eyes
    5. Skin around eyes red
    6. Black teeth
    7. Milky-white tongue
  B. Possible Names
    1. "Red-eyed" lizard
    2. "Black-toothed" lizard
    3. "White-tongued" lizard

  C. Habitat
    1. Predatory birds
    2. Up to 20 lizards live together
    3. Deep holes
  D. Food
    1. Small animals
    2. Insects
    3. Certain cactus thorns
    4. Shells of sunflower seeds

10. On subsequent days, have students work together (without your direct guidance) and then individually to create outlines for additional chapters.

CLASSIFYING, CATEGORIZING, AND PRIORITIZING

Explanation

Like the previous lesson on outlining, this one engages students in sorting out concepts and prioritizing information. Students work kinesthetically—with both a pocket chart and with cards spread out on the floor—to order ideas from broad to specific.

Skill Focus

Classifying and categorizing; paraphrasing and summarizing using main ideas, events, details, and themes; clarifying main ideas and details; skimming and scanning

Materials & Resources

Text

- For modeling: A chapter or section of a science or social studies textbook (Used in this lesson: the chapter "Rocks and Minerals" from *Earth Science*, Harcourt Science)

- For students' work: a comparable content area textbook chapter

Other

- Prepared index cards (see Prior to the Lesson)

- Pocket chart

Prior to the Lesson: For both the text you'll be using for whole-class work and for the text students will use for group work, identify the headings and key details. Write each on an individual index card. For student group work, you'll need several sets of each word card.

STEPS

1. Tell students that today's lesson focuses on the skills of classifying/ categorizing and prioritizing. Explain that classifying/categorizing involves identifying common elements and grouping by these commonalities. Prioritizing means arranging the groups in a hierarchy, typically from the broadest group to the smallest. (If you've used the lesson on outlining, refer to this as a good example of prioritizing.)

2. At the top of a transparency or the board, write the word *Cars*. Tell students this is the overall category, or topic. Call on volunteers to come up with different types of cars—for example, sedan, minivan, or SUV. List three in a row, underneath *Cars*. Continue by having students identify specific models for each of those categories and write these model names below the car types. Emphasize to students that what they've just done is to create a hierarchy, with each level broader or more important than the level underneath.

3. Now call attention to the prepared index cards and the pocket chart. Tell students that these are headings and key words from a science chapter. Place the cards, with words visible, randomly in the chart.

4. Enlist students' help in arranging the cards in a hierarchy. Guide them by asking questions such as, "What's the broadest category among all these words and concepts?" or "What concept(s) flow directly from that category?" A completed example for a pocket chart based on the sample text is on the following page.

On a table, randomly lay out an assortment of writing instruments (for example: 10 pencils—some sharpened, some not sharpened, some red, some regular lead; 5 pens; 6 crayons; 6 markers). Have students come up with categories (color, height, type, purpose, and so on) and group the items accordingly. Have them explain the reasoning they used to make the categorization.

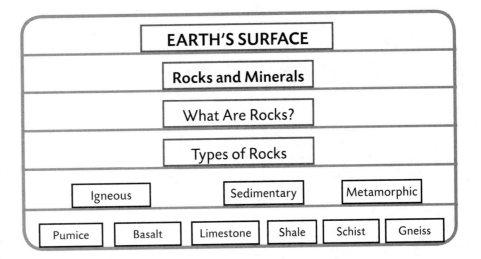

5. Set up small groups. Give each group a set of identical cards based on another chapter. Instruct groups to organize the cards into correct categories and classifications in a hierarchical structure. Invite students to use the floor to spread out and arrange their cards.

6. When all are finished, have students walk around the room to see what different groups have done. Engage the class in a discussion about the groups' work.

USING A TABLE OF CONTENTS AS A HIERARCHICAL SYSTEM

STEPS

1. Review the concept of hierarchy that students have been working with in the previous two lessons. Have volunteers offer definitions of classifying/categorizing and of prioritizing information. Tell students that in this lesson you'll show them how the hierarchical system is used in all of their textbooks—math, science, social studies, history, and others—in a prominent place that is already familiar. Ask if anyone can guess what it is. Guide students to realize that you are referring to the table of contents.

2. On the board or a transparency, draw the following diagram of a hierarchical system to illustrate how information may be organized in a chapter of text.

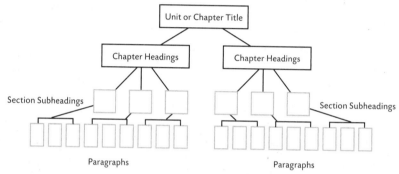

3. Explain to students how this system is used to organize almost all chapters of a text, going from overall topic to very specific details.

4. Distribute a copy of the preselected content area textbook to each student. of the hierarchical system can help them to locate broad informational categories quickly and efficiently by using the table of contents. (Point out that a table of contents does not include the paragraph/detail level.)

5. Pose questions and challenge students to use only the table of contents to respond. Below is a set of example questions and answers, based on the sample text:

   • At about what page will I find the first mention of information about ecosystems? (*Title/introductory page: "Looking at Ecosystems," p. B2*)

   • Where am I likely to find out what a niche is? (*Chapter: "Ecosystems"; Subheading: "What Are Habitats and Niches?" p. B18*)

   • Where am I likely to find out the location of tropical rain forests? (*Subheading: "What are Tropical Rain Forests and Coral Reefs?" p. B24*)

   • Where is information on conserving ecosystems? (*Subheading: "What is Conservation?" p. B84*)

6. Conclude by having students explain in their own words why hierarchical organization is so important and used so frequently in textbooks.

Using Text Features and Organizers

The manner in which text is organized, arranged, and presented to the reader is far from arbitrary. Especially in informational text, but in drama, poetry, and fiction as well, authors and editors purposefully include elements to help readers navigate texts. Too often, however, students of all ages overlook even obvious text signals. As teachers, we can address this situation by providing effective direct instruction in how to use these kinds of features.

Potentially helpful text signals abound. Books are divided into logical sections to help readers focus on specifics. Tables of contents and indexes help readers locate those specifics more efficiently so that they do not have to wade through pages of irrelevant material. Chapters, headings, and subheadings are provided to categorize and prioritize material. Special effects—such as boldfaced or italicized words, photo captions, or sidebar boxes—are also used to enhance presentation of important material.

The lessons in this section are all aimed at helping students build a comfort level that will allow them to move from genre to genre and text to text with confidence and proficiency. Because content reading is important at these upper grades, several lessons help heighten students' awareness of the text signals that editors and authors use to organize informational text. Students will also identify and compare different genres—from folktales to biographies—by exploring their characteristics. They will also journey far into the depths of text. You'll be taking out your "scalpel" to dissect a rollicking poem through which students will learn about tone, rhyme, and the technical terms of poetry. You'll also help them explore the interior of texts to search for seven different internal text structures, for narrative techniques of foreshadowing and flashback, and for Internet text savvy.

Our goal throughout is to help students improve their reading and understanding by giving them a better grasp of the uniqueness of the many text structures and signals that are there to help them. We cannot assume that they will see the obvious. Our job, as in so much of education, is to help them find the way.

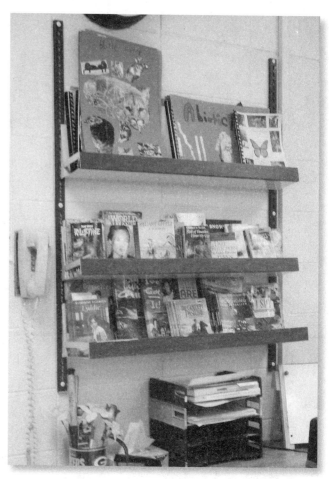

A classroom library that offers a variety of books and text materials is a great way to expose students to different genres.

This girl is identifying the elements of a popular fairy tale. Reading comprehension is increased when students understand the structural elements of both informational text and narrative text.

DISSECTING A POEM

Prior to the Lesson: If you choose to use a doctor's lab coat, and a doctor kit as well, prepare these materials ahead of time.

STEPS

1. Start this lesson with great fanfare, explaining that you're a doctor today. Say something like, "Boys and girls, I have some surgery to perform this morning. Let me see if my patient is ready."

2. Display the transparency of the preselected poem. "I've got to perform a 'stanzadectomy,' which means I have to remove a stanza. I'm planning to remove one that has something different from the others." Explain that a *stanza* is a group of lines that is much like a paragraph in prose. Stanzas have spaces between them. Go through the poem to identify several stanzas.

3. Tell students that first you need to check for a heartbeat or *rhythm*. Using your real or pretend stethoscope, read several lines and count the beats. Now use an "instrument" (your red transparency pen) to mark the beats (stressed and unstressed syllables). Employ the customary symbols to mark stressed and unstressed syllables. For the sample poem, your marks would look like this:

```
u /   u /    u   /   u  /
I do / not like / green eggs / and ham.

u /   u /    u    /   u /
I do / not like / them, Sam / -I-am.
```

4. Comment that the patient seems to have a regular, even heartbeat. You might ask students to help you count the beats in the other stanzas so that they get a feel for the rhythm and can identify whether it changes.

5. Call attention to the *rhyming pattern* in the lines you have displayed. For the sample poem, most of the lines have an *end rhyme* with an *AABB pattern*. Use your red pen to mark this pattern on the transparency.

6. Next, tell students that your scan of the "patient" has revealed a *refrain*. Tell students that this is a line or a couple of lines repeated throughout a poem for effect. For the sample poem, the refrain is shown in Step 3.

Bonus Ideas

Have on hand several oversized white shirts for students to use as lab coats. Let them take over the role of doctor to dissect another poem. (Provide several possibilities; try other Dr. Seuss books or any number of other humorous poems with nonsensical and vivid wordplay.) Organize them into small groups to practice, then have them perform "surgery" in front of the class.

7. Now inform students that you're ready to perform the operation. You're looking for a particular stanza. For the sample poem, this stanza includes—in addition to the end rhyme pattern—*internal rhyme*. Search through the poem to find the stanza that is different. Use your scissors to cut it out of the transparency and display it on the overhead. With your red marker, underline the internally rhyming words in this stanza. For the sample, the stanza you would remove occurs in the middle of the poem and includes two sets of internal rhyme: *would not, could not* in the first line and *house* and *mouse* in the fifth and sixth lines.

8. Now inform students that your one last probe as a surgeon is to find the *tone* of the patient. Using your green pen, locate and underline clues that indicate the tone. For the sample poem, the tone is comical and lighthearted. Clues might be: nonsensical words, silly rhymes, and a humorous topic.

9. Declare your surgery to remove a stanza with internal rhyme—that is, your stanzadectomy!—a success. Now review the poetic terms students have learned: refrain, stanza, tone, rhythm, rhyme, internal rhyme, end rhyme, rhyming pattern (AABB).

INTERNAL TEXT STRUCTURE: 7 TYPES

Explanation

Students need to look carefully at the internal structure of texts to understand them to a greater degree. This lesson explores some of the most common types of internal structure. Students' knowledge of different purposes served by different structures should also help them incorporate these elements into their own writing.

Skill Focus

Using the internal organization of text to improve comprehension: compare and contrast, listing, cause and effect, description, problem and solution, question and answer, and sequential order

Materials & Resources

Text

*   A text representing several of the structures explored in this lesson (Used in this lesson: *The Journey* by Sarah Stewart)

*   A science or social studies text with a question-and-answer format

Other

*   7 sentence strips and 1 envelope per small group (see Prior to the Lesson)

*   Chart paper or posterboard

Bonus Ideas

In subsequent readings of any text, stop and identify the internal text structure. Refer to the choices listed on the chart created in this lesson. Write the titles that represent these various structures on the chart to correspond with the structure. Students can refer to this chart on an ongoing basis.

Prior to the Lesson: Type a set of sentences on a sheet of paper. (Each sentence should represent a different text pattern.) Make a copy for each set of partners or small group. Cut apart each sentence on a separate strip and package each group of seven strips in an envelope. A set of sample sentences is at right.

STEPS

1. Explain to students that authors organize their writing around specific text structures, or patterns. These structures help the reader navigate the text smoothly and make sense of what is happening. As you talk briefly about the seven types of internal structure covered in this lesson (listed in Skill Focus) write on chart paper or posterboard what each of the terms means. Many of the relationships will be self-explanatory, but some will require discussion.

2. Ask students to think about these relationships as they apply to sentences. Set up partners or small groups. Give each group an envelope containing the prepared sentence strips. Ask them to discuss each strip and to reach consensus about the relationship it illustrates; tell them they should look at the chart to remind themselves of their choices. Ask them to be prepared to defend their decision and to write the relationship on the back of each strip.

3. After approximately 10–15 minutes, have each group read aloud one strip and state what they feel it represents. Encourage discussion and debate among groups who disagree.

4. Now show students the preselected book, read aloud representative sections, and help students identify the predominant text structure(s). Discuss how and why the structure is an effective basis for organizing the book. For example, the sample book is clearly built around comparing and contrasting, in journal-style, the big city life experienced by a young Amish girl with her small-town lifestyle.

5. As time allows on this or a subsequent day, call attention to different expository text structures in a science or social studies book. For example, many content area textbooks use questions as headings, with answers appearing in the text that follows. Discuss how this format helps readers to both frame and remember important text points.

> Some people like rock music while some people like country.
>
> There are numerous types of music: rock, country, rap, jazz, blues, heavy metal, classical, folk, hip hop, reggae, and opera, among many others.
>
> Classical music is usually thought of as formal and complex, dating as far back as the year 1000 A.D., but is still created today.
>
> Music companies are sponsoring legislation to prevent the distribution of music on the Internet without the purchase of this music.
>
> Hip hop music started as disco rap in the 1970s, and rock started in the 1950s with rock and roll and rockabilly.
>
> The British Invasion, an age of Beatlemania, resulted in many new rock musicians.
>
> In an attempt to copy the idolized Beatles, many musicians began to produce cheap recordings in informal studios. This music came to be known as "garage rock."
>
> What music had its roots in New Orleans? Jazz was born in New Orleans from a blend of spirituals, blues, and ragtime beats.

TWO-PART LESSON: USING TEXT FEATURES

PART 1: RECOGNIZING TEXT SIGNALS

⦿ Explanation

Text signals such as headings, key words, and captions are placed throughout text by editors, authors, and publishers to help readers prioritize, absorb, and remember information. But unless these visual cues are pointed out and explained to students, they may not see the obvious. This lesson shows students how to effectively preview a text by using these signals.

⦿ Skill Focus

Using text features, such as headings, subheadings, and key words; summarizing main ideas and details

⦿ Materials & Resources

Text

- A chapter of a content area textbook (science or social studies/history) on a topic about which students know very little

Other

- Blank transparency
- Colored chalk or transparency markers

⦿ Bonus Ideas

Capitalize on the competitive nature of your students by calling for Preview Challenges on occasion. Organize students in small groups. Give each group a piece of paper. Tell them that when you give the word, they are to turn to the chapter you assign and quickly preview the text signals. When your timer goes off (after about two minutes), they are to close their books. The winning team is the one that has created the most detailed, organized web.

STEPS

1. Explain that good readers are always sorting through text and organizing information by levels of importance. They are aware that they can do a better job of sorting and organizing if they look for and use the many text signals that authors, editors, and publishers provide.

2. Ask students what they know about a particular topic (a topic you've chosen deliberately because you know it is unfamiliar to students). Write the topic in the middle of the board. Ask students to begin by sharing what they already know (or think they know) about the topic. Create a topic map as students volunteer information. An example for the topic Thermal Energy follows:

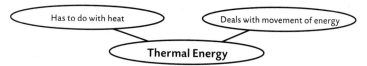

3. Explain to students that you'll now be going to a textbook chapter that focuses on the topic of thermal energy: the class is embarking on a visual experiment that will help them find a lot of information simply by keeping their eyes open (and staying alert, of course!). On the board near the topic map, draw an eye and alongside it write "Eye Clues." Open to a double-page spread that includes a chapter title and multiple visual text features.

4. Ask students to help you identify those things that readily catch their attention. List them on the board as categories under the Eye Clues heading. With your guidance, responses should include categories like Big/Bold Print, Colors, Illustrations, Captions, Underlining, Italics, Bullets.

5. Distribute a book to each student. Tell them they have about two minutes to preview the chapter on Thermal Energy. Instead of reading it, you want them only to look at the eye-catching signals on the pages. Set a timer and have them focus on the pictures, the captions, and highlighted text.

6. When time is up, have students close their books. Return to the topic map you've drawn. Call on volunteers to tell you what they've learned. With a different-color marker or chalk, add all the information they can recall.

7. Now have students go through the section again, actually reading it this time. Remind them that their preview of text features has provided a great framework from which to operate; they now better know what to look for.

8. Return to the web after this reading and, with a third color of marker or chalk, add the newest information to the map.

TWO-PART LESSON: USING TEXT FEATURES

PART 2: USING TEXT SIGNALS TO PREVIEW TEXT

Explanation

Now that students have expanded their awareness of the major text signals, this lesson will give them a more methodical way of previewing text using those same features. As you guide students with a think-aloud using a graphic organizer, students see how asking the right questions and looking for the right text signals can greatly improve their comprehension.

Skill Focus

Using text features: headings, subheadings, illustrations, titles, and keywords; summarizing main ideas and details

Materials & Resources

Text

- A content area textbook: science, social studies/history, math, or health (Used in this lesson: the chapter, "Water in the Oceans," from *Earth Science*, Harcourt Science)

Other

- Text Preview organizer (see Appendix, p. 124), 1 copy per student

- Transparency of Text Preview organizer

- Colored transparency markers

Bonus Ideas

- Have students use the organizer as an effective homework sheet. They will see it as quick and easy, and they'll also soon realize how prepared they are for a discussion without having done extensive reading.

STEPS

1. Display the transparency of the Text Preview organizer and keep the textbook you're using handy. Review the "eye signals" presented in the Part 1 lesson by checking them or underlining them on the transparency as you talk about them briefly. Tell students you'll show them how to preview text today using these signals in a way that will greatly aid their comprehension.

2. Find the title of the chapter and condense it into only a few words, unless this has already been done. Write the words on the top line. Now ask yourself: "What do I already know about this topic?" Brainstorm aloud, saying, "Okay, the title of the chapter is 'Water in the Oceans.' Well, I know a good bit about oceans since I vacation at the beach every year. I would like to learn more about ocean currents since I know they can be dangerous to swimmers." (Keep your comments brief, since it's only a preview.)

3. Now drop to the next level, Heading. Glance through several pages and skim the headings. Find just three to copy on the lines provided. With each, ask: "What do I think is the relationship between this heading and the topic?" For the heading "What Role Do Oceans Play in the Water Cycle?" you might say, "I know the basics of the water cycle, evaporation and condensation. I'm sure it'll deal with that concept."

4. For the next level, Picture Walk, look through the chapter to find visuals—charts, graphs, photos, drawings—and decide on three to replicate. Read any accompanying captions. Do a simple sketch of each, asking: "How do I think this connects to the topic?" In response, add a few words underneath your pictures to capture the essence of the connection.

5. Continue to the next level. Choose four highlighted words that say something crucial about the topic. As you jot down each, ask: "How do I think this connects to the topic?" Answer briefly in your think-aloud.

6. For the next line, tell students you'll have a chance to show your natural curiosity about something related to the text by completing the sentence, "I wonder . . .." You might say, "Okay, since this section is called 'Getting Fresh Water from Salt Water,' I wonder why we don't get more of our fresh drinking water from the ocean."

7. Tell students that you're now ready to respond to the last line that says: "This is mainly about…." Capture your summary with only a few words—for example, ". . . how oceans provide a large amount of Earth's fresh water."

8. Distribute an organizer to each student. Have them follow your model to fill in the form during assigned content area reading.

IDENTIFYING FORESHADOWING

Explanation

Foreshadowing is a writing technique used mostly in narrative text to allow the reader to make assumptions about what will take place later in the text. Proficient readers are attuned to this and are prepared for what will occur. By piquing their interest through talking about foreshadowing in scary movies (a favorite film genre of this age group), you'll also likely achieve your goal of teaching them about an important literary technique.

Skill Focus

Identifying foreshadowing technique; understanding internal structure and organization of text

Materials & Resources

Text

- Any grade-appropriate text that uses foreshadowing (Used in this lesson: *Encounter* by Jane Yolen)

Other

- Blank transparency
- Transparency marker; chalk
- 1 sheet of paper for each student

Bonus Ideas

- Remind students during writing time that foreshadowing is a technique they may wish to try.
- Try playing some classical music clips to let students decide which selections would make good foreshadowing music for suspense movies. Which selections change tempo to indicate that the direction of the plot is changing? Perhaps some ambitious students could write a script to match it.

STEPS

1. Ask your students who among them watches scary movies (most will likely raise their hands), and pose this question: "What occurs just before something really scary is about to happen? How does the movie alert you to be prepared for something scary?" They will likely respond that there's a certain eerie music that plays and sometimes the scene is dark.

2. Tell students that this technique used is called *foreshadowing*—letting you know beforehand that something is about to happen. Authors use the same technique in their writing, but, of course, there's no possibility of their using music or lighting effects. Instead, they use words in clever, distinct ways. Today you'll model how this works in text.

3. On the board or a transparency, create four columns—one to record clues the author has provided as part of the foreshadowing; one to note the event that has been foreshadowed; and the other two to record page numbers. Title the columns as shown in Step 4.

4. Display the preselected text and read it aloud once for enjoyment. Then go back through the text to model how you identify examples of foreshadowing. Call attention to both the text clues and the event that has been foreshadowed. Fill in the columns as you think aloud. For the sample book, the chart might look like this:

Clues That Make Us Suspicious (i.e., Foreshadowing)	Page	Event	Page
Clap of thunder awaking natives from a bad dream of three winged birds with voices like thunder and sharp, white teeth	1	Arrival of three ships	2
Eyes blue and gray like the shifting sea	15	Soon the kindness of the visitors shifted, and the natives' lives would soon change and shift, too.	21
Strangers touched golden nose rings and golden armbands but not the flesh of natives' faces or arms.	15	The visitors later took natives' gold and treated them inhumanely.	21

5. Distribute a sheet of paper to each student. Have them draw columns to create a chart like the one you modeled. Using an assigned or independent reading book, students should read to find evidence of foreshadowing and record it on their chart.

INVESTIGATING THE INTERNET

The Internet can be a great reference tool for students but it must be approached with the knowledge that not all information out there is accurate or useful information. Because students depend on the Internet to locate information for many reasons, they need to be able to evaluate the credibility of a given Web site. In this lesson, students brainstorm what makes for a legitimate, high-quality Web site and then go on to actually evaluate Web sites. Note: You might use this lesson in conjunction with two Section 3 lessons, pages 49–51.

Skill Focus

Using reference aids: thesaurus, atlas, dictionary, Internet, glossary, table of contents, index; using electronic sources to access information; reading and navigating Internet and media text; detecting bias, propaganda techniques, stereotypes, and exaggeration

Materials & Resources

Text

- Web sites related to content area curriculum

Other

- Web pages copied onto transparencies and/or computer access
- Chart paper
- Markers

Prior to the Lesson: Find a range of sites—excellent to poor (with all, of course, approved and appropriate for student use). Copy select pages (home pages and internal pages) onto transparencies. Also, prepare a list of appropriate Web sites for students to evaluate online.

STEPS

1. Explain that there is a lot of factual-looking material on the Internet—anyone can put something up and design it in a slick way so that it "looks" credible—but it doesn't mean any bona fide research is behind it. (If you have used the lessons on pages 49–51, this would be a good time to review students' work with spoof Web sites.) Explain, too, that Web sites vary in quality—some may contain credible information, but they may be poorly organized, hard to understand, and so on.

2. Now post the blank chart paper and, along with students, brainstorm a list of items they think will help prove that the information on a given Web site is of high quality and reliable. At right are items/questions you should aim to include in the list.

   - What is the domain of the site? (Point out that information from .edu and gov is the most likely to be trusted and useful for student research.)
       - edu = education site
       - gov = government site
       - org = organization site
       - com = commercial site
       - net = network infrastructure site
   - Is the site at your readability level?
   - Does the site cover your topic better than other sites?
   - Who is responsible for the site? What are their credentials?
   - Does the site clearly differentiate between facts and opinions?
   - Is the site trying to persuade you to buy something?
   - Are there any spelling or grammatical errors on the page?
   - Does the page contain lots of information that is clutter-free (i.e., well organized and easily accessible)?
   - Is the information up-to-date?

3. With these questions in mind, display a Web site transparency you've prepared. Together with students, read through the transparency and have them look for items listed on the chart paper. Evaluate the site based on the chart criteria. Invite students to give the Web site a grade on a scale of 1–3. (A score of 3 means the site meets all or most of the criteria; 2 means half of the criteria; and 1 means few, if any, criteria are met.)

4. Finally, display several additional prepared transparencies. (Or, alternately, provide a list of preselected Web sites and have students sit at computers.) Have students work in pairs to evaluate each site. Alert them to be careful—not all sites are top quality! Invite the class to share results afterward.

IDENTIFYING FLASHBACK

Explanation

While the technique of flashback can make for a more complex, interesting narrative, it can also cause confusion if students don't understand what the technique is or how to look for it. This lesson helps them understand how narrative text makes use of flashback and it gives students a chance to practice finding it.

Skill Focus

Identifying flashback, plot within a plot, and chronological order in narrative text; using the internal organization of text to improve comprehension, coding text

Materials & Resources

Text

- Multiple copies of any grade-appropriate text with flashbacks (Used in this lesson: *Holes* by Louis Sachar)

Other

- Photographs of an event from when you were young

- A sticky note cut into VIP strips for each student

- Posterboard or temporary photo album

- Tape or glue to attach photos to posterboard

Bonus Ideas

Charlie and the Chocolate Factory has some great flashbacks from Willie Wonka's childhood. Show your class a clip from this movie as an introduction or a supplement to this lesson.

Prior to the Lesson: Gather some photos from when you were young to illustrate a story you will tell as you introduce the concept of flashback. Either place them in a temporary album to pass around the classroom or mount them on posterboard so that students can come up to view them. (You may want to make copies of the photos to use for this activity.)

STEPS

1. Explain to students that today you're going to talk about the technique of flashback and how it's used in stories. Tell the class you'll define *flashback* in a moment but first they should listen carefully as you tell them a story about something that happened to you recently. A sample story follows:

   Yesterday I took Phoebe, my dog, to the Versailles State Park. We hiked the trails and waded through the small creeks. I put some treats in my pocket to give her while we were on our walk. As we were walking I began to think...

2. Now bring out the pictures of when you were young and complete your story. (You could pass them around in an album you've prepared or have them mounted on a posterboard and let students come up to look at them before you begin.) Tell the students a story about the photos you brought. A sample story follows:

   At 8 years of age, I took my dog, Lady, to the North Vernon City Park. I walked her across the street at the stoplight a few blocks down the road from my house. After strolling through one of the empty baseball fields, I unleashed her. I threw the ball and Frisbee for her to retrieve.

3. Tell students that at the end of the first story, you had a flashback. Explain that a flashback is a description of something that happened in the past, a memory of a past event. It can be triggered by doing something very similar to what you did in the past, or it can even be triggered by something more abstract: a smell, a certain color, or a sound.

4. Tell students that in stories authors write flashbacks within their stories to give background knowledge, to move the story along, or to establish a purpose for a character's actions. Explain that it's important for them to understand this technique when reading a story. They need to be able to identify flashback and pay close attention when it is happening, or they could become confused and lose the thread of the story.

5. Distribute copies of the preselected text and give each student a sticky note cut into VIP strips. Tell them to place the strips in the text where they notice a flashback. Alert students about what to expect within the text you are using. In the sample text, there are numerous flashbacks.

6. When students finish reading, discuss the flashbacks and their purpose within the text.

Two-Part Lesson: Characteristics of Genres

Part 1: Identifying Literary Genres

○ Explanation

Most students have been exposed to the genres they will survey in this and the next lesson. However, they may not know how to define each genre, nor realize how much the genre affects the nature of a text. This lesson lays out the characteristics of various common literary genres and helps students organize their observations by using a matrix. With minor modifications, this lesson may be taught a few times to include other types of genres—for example, biography, poetry, and technical writing.

○ Skill Focus

Identifying differences among various forms of fiction; identifying types and characteristics of genres; using graphic organizers; comparing and contrasting themes; classifying and categorizing ideas

○ Materials & Resources

Text

• Classroom basal with different genre examples flagged, or books representing each of several different genres (5 different genres work well)

• Familiar fairy tale

Other

• Genre Matrix (see Appendix, p. 125), 1 photocopy for each student

• Transparency of Genre Matrix

• Characteristics of Literary Genres handout, 1 photocopy for each student

• Index cards, 1 for each student

Prior to the Lesson: Use the boxed material on page 116 as the basis for creating a handout titled "Characteristics of Literary Genres." Make one photocopy for each student. (Note: the material is not intended to be a comprehensive listing; instead, it should be seen as a springboard for fleshing out your own list.)

STEPS

1. Begin this lesson with a discussion of genre and some of the types of literary, or fiction, genres students are familiar with or will be introduced to. Explain that each genre has its own unique set of characteristics that help you to identify it and to understand why the story might progress as it does. Give examples of the characteristics of some favorite student genres: For example, fantasy may include talking animals and magic, while mysteries are suspenseful and focus around a character who solves a crime.

2. Explain that students will be previewing books in five different literary genres. Introduce each text students will look at today: Identify the genre and its special characteristics, show the cover and first section, and give a little background knowledge.

3. Distribute an index card to each student.

4. Now place the books in stations around the classroom, divide the class into five groups, and give students time to preview each book. Tell students to write down the title of each book on their index card as soon as they arrive at a station. Then, instruct them to look at each book's illustrations, read as much of the text as they can, and/or discuss the book with their group. Set a timer for two to four minutes, then rotate the groups.

5. Once all students have previewed each book, have them look at their note card and number the titles in order, number 1 being the text they want to read first.

6. Collect the index cards and tell the students you will assign them to a group for tomorrow's reading.

7. Distribute a copy of the Genre Matrix (Appendix, p. 125) to each student. Tell students to use the first column to list the five different genres they previewed and the title of each corresponding book. Also, give each student a copy of the genre characteristics handout at this time.

8. Next, display the transparency of the Matrix. Using a preselected familiar fairy tale, model how you fill in the remaining columns for that story. Have students follow along—without doing any further writing—on their own forms.

9. Collect each student's matrix and characteristics handout and tell the class they will get to fill out their own matrix in tomorrow's lesson.

Characteristics of Literary Genres

Realistic Fiction
- set in modern time
- events could really happen
- characters seem like people you could meet in real life

Historical Fiction
- happens in the past
- setting is often real
- some events based on real events in history
- some characters might be historical, but most are made-up

Fantasy
- make-believe atmosphere
- may include talking animals and magic
- fantastic, unrealistic events occur

Myth
- explains something about the world
- involves gods or other supernatural beings

Mystery
- usually realistic
- suspenseful
- includes an event not explained until the end
- involves solving a crime
- centered around a character who investigates wrongdoing

Fable
- short narrative
- makes a point or teaches a lesson
- often involves talking animals

Legend
- may tell about real people or events but not verified to be true
- may involve exaggeration
- passed down from earlier times

Science Fiction
- happens in the future or in another dimension
- includes some fact and fictional elements
- often takes place in outer space

Fairy Tale
- often involves royalty
- usually has a happy ending
- characters typically include witches, ogres, giants, elves, fairies, and dragons
- magical things usually happen

TWO-PART LESSON: CHARACTERISTICS OF GENRES

PART 2: USING GENRE CHARACTERISTICS TO MAKE COMPARISONS

Explanation

Now that students have become somewhat familiar with the characteristics of various genres, they will continue filling in their matrixes and use information from the matrix to compare and contrast various types of literature. Teach this lesson several times to ensure various genres are analyzed.

Skill Focus

Identifying differences among various forms of fiction; identifying types and characteristics of genres; identifying characteristics of poetry, narrative, expository, technical, and persuasive writing; using graphic organizers; comparing and contrasting themes; classifying and categorizing ideas

Materials & Resources

Text

- Classroom basal with different genre examples flagged, or books representing each of several different genres (5 different genres work well)

- Several books within each of the genres discussed in the "Book Guess"

Other

- Students' matrixes from Part 1 of this lesson

- Transparency of Genre Matrix from Part 1

- Index cards from Part 1

- Sticky notes cut into VIP strips, 2 for each student

Prior to the Lesson: *Use the index cards from Part 1 to assign each student to one of the five different genre groups.*

STEPS

1. Begin by briefly discussing yesterday's lesson on literary genres and their characteristics. Then tell students you'll start this lesson with a review and a challenge: a "Book Guess." Show students several different books and have them guess the genre and describe its special characteristics.

2. Hand back to each student his or her partially filled-in matrix (from the Part 1 lesson) and genre characteristics list. Organize students into five small groups (see Prior to the Lesson) and distribute the appropriate text to each group. Also, give each student two sticky notes cut into VIP strips.

3. Tell students to read one page at a time. After each page, the group should discuss any special characteristics of their genre that occur on that page and place a VIP strip in the text to mark the characteristic.

4. When they are finished, the group should work together to fill in the row that goes along with their book.

5. At this time, you might want to conclude the lesson and have the students read a different genre the next day, filling out another row of their matrix, or you might go on to Steps 6 and 7.

6. Gather the whole class and display the transparency from Part 1. Have each group present their row of the matrix. As they describe their row, discuss and correct the information if necessary and then write it on your transparency. Have all students simultaneously record the same information on their matrix.

7. When finished, ask questions such as the following:

   - What's the difference between the characters in a fairy tale and those in a myth?

   - What's one primary difference between realistic fiction and historical fiction?

   - What are the similarities between legend and science fiction? Differences?

CHARACTERS I'VE MET

Character: _____

○ Main character

○ Minor character

My sketch:

Things I know about this character: _____

_____

_____

_____

_____

Character: _____

○ Main character

○ Minor character

My sketch:

Things I know about this character: _____

_____

_____

_____

_____

Character: _____

○ Main character

○ Minor character

My sketch:

Things I know about this character: _____

_____

_____

_____

_____

CHARACTER CLUES

Character's Name	What the Character Does	What the Character Says	What Others/Speaker Say About the Character
Main Character			
Character 1			
Character 2			
Character 3			

Summary of Main Character: _____

_____

Summary of Character 1: _____

_____

Summary of Character 2: _____

_____

Summary of Character 3: _____

_____

DOUBLE-ENTRY RESPONSE JOURNAL

The text says . . .	I think . . .

CHARACTER ANALYSIS CHART

Name of Character: _____

Team Name: _____

Proof (page #)					
Our Notes					

SEQUENTIAL LOG

As you read, write the main events in order.

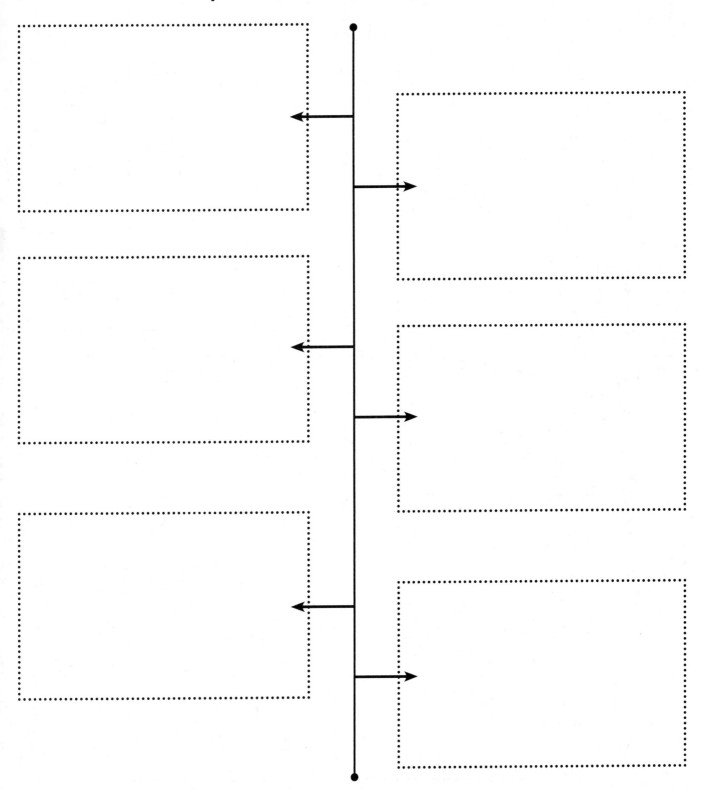

COMPARE/CONTRAST MATRIX

Title and Author	Characters	Setting	Problem	Solution	Illustrations
Title of Story: Author:					
Title of Story: Author:					
Title of Story: Author:					
Title of Story: Author:					
Title of Story: Author:					

CREATING MENTAL IMAGES

Name _____   Pages/Chapters Read _____

Title _____   Author _____

In each box below sketch a mental image you formed during reading.

1.	2.	3.
4.	5.	6.

Write descriptive words from the story that correspond with your mental images. Write the page number on which you found the words. Then write the sense your image reflects.

Passage	Page #	Sense
1.		
2.		
3.		
4.		
5.		
6.		

TEXT PREVIEW ORGANIZER

Title: _____

Heading: _____

Heading: _____

Heading: _____

Picture Walk

[ ]	[ ]	[ ]

What is the picture telling you?
_____
_____

What is the picture telling you?
_____
_____

What is the picture telling you?
_____
_____

I think these words are important: _____

I wonder _____

This is mainly about _____

GENRE MATRIX

	Special Characteristics of the Genre	Setting	Characters	Plot
Title: Genre:				
Title: Genre:				
Title: Genre:				
Title: Genre:				
Title: Genre:				

Arnold, T. (1997). *Parts*. New York: Dial Books for Young Readers.

Arnold, T. (2001). *More parts*. New York: Dial Books for Young Readers.

Arnold, T. (2004). *Even more parts*. New York: Dial Books for Young Readers.

Ausubel, D. P., Novak, J., & Hanesian, H. (1978). *Educational psychology: A cognitive view* (2nd ed.). New York: Holt, Rhinehart & Winston.

Barnidge, T. (2003). *Whiz Kid Quarterbacks*. New York: DK Publishing, Inc.

Boehm, R., et. al. (2000). Harcourt Brace Social Studies, *Early United States*. Orlando, FL: Harcourt Brace & Co.

Borduin, B. J., Borduin, C. M., & Manley, C. M. (1994). The use of imagery training to improve reading comprehension of second graders. *The Journal of Genetic Psychology, 155*(1), 115–118.

Bradby, M. (1995). *More than anything else*. New York: Orchard Books.

Brain, M. *How sleep works*. Retrieved January 2007 from HowStuffWorks: http://health.howstuffworks.com/sleep.htm

Bransford, J., Franks, J., Vye, N., & Sherwood, R. (1989). *New approaches to instruction: Because wisdom can't be told*. New York: Cambridge University Press.

Bromley, K., Irwin-De Vitis, L., & Modlo, M. (1995). *Graphic organizers: Visual strategies for active learning*. New York: Scholastic.

Brooks, J. G. (2004). To see beyond the lesson. *Educational Leadership, 62*(1), 8–12.

Brown, M. W. (1949). *The important book*. New York: HarperCollins Publishers.

Carnegie Council on Adolescent Development. (1995). *Great transitions: Preparing adolescents for a new century*. New York: Carnegie Corporation.

Climo, S. (1989). *The Egyptian Cinderella*. New York: HarperCollins Children's Books.

Climo, S. (1993). *The Korean Cinderella*. New York: HarperTrophy.

Climo, S. (1996). *The Irish Cinderlad*. New York: HarperTrophy.

Col, J. George Crum: Inventor of potato chips. Retrieved December 2006 from Enchanted Learning: http://www.enchantedlearning.com

Cunningham, J. (2007, January 14). Speech at Four-Blocks Leadership Workshop. Winston-Salem, NC.

Deedy, C. A. (2000). *The yellow star: The legend of King Christian X of Denmark*. Atlanta, GA: Peachtree Publishers.

de Maupassant, G. The necklace. In Brander Matthews (Ed.), *The short-story: Specimens illustrating its development*. Retrieved December 2006 from Bartleby.com: www.bartleby.com/195/20.htm.

Dole, J. A., Duffy, G.G., Roehler, L.R. & Pearson, P.D. (1991). Moving from the old to the new: Research on reading comprehension instruction. *Review of Educational Research, 61*, 239-264.

Dr. Seuss. (1960). *Green eggs and ham*. New York: Random House Books for Young Readers.

Durkin, D. (1993). *Teaching them to read* (6th ed.). Boston: Allyn & Bacon.

Fletcher, R. (1998). *Flying solo*. New York: Dell Yearling.

Frank, M., et. al. (2000). Harcourt Science, Grade 4, *Earth science*. Orlando, FL: Harcourt School Publishers.

Fredericks, A. (1999). *Animal sharpshooters*. New York: Franklin Watts.

Funke, C. (2005). *Inkspell*. Somerset, UK: The Chicken House.

Gambrell, L. B., & Koskinen, P. S. (2002). Imagery: A strategy for enhancing comprehension. In C. C. Block & M. Pressley (Eds.), *Comprehension instruction: Research-based best practices*. New York: Guilford Press.

Garland, S. *The lotus seed*. (1993). San Diego, CA: Harcourt Brace & Co.

Harris, R. (2000). Evaluating Internet research sources. In *A guide to the web*. Guilford, CT: Dushkin/McGraw-Hill.

Harris, T. L., & Hodges, R. E. (Eds.). (1995). *The literacy dictionary: The vocabulary of reading and writing*. Newark, DE: International Reading Association.

Harvey, S., & Goudvis, A. (2000). *Strategies that work: Teaching comprehension to enhance understanding*. Portland, ME: Stenhouse Publishers.

Hoyt, L. (1999). *Revisit, reflect, retell: Strategies for improving reading comprehension*. Portsmouth, NH: Heinemann.

Hyerle, D. (1996). *Visual tools for constructing knowledge*. Alexandria, VA: Association for Supervision and Curriculum Development (ASCD).

Jamestown Education. (2001). The world's wildest horse race. In *The wild side: Extreme sports*. New York: Glencoe/McGraw-Hill.

Johnston, T. *The harmonica*. (2004). Watertown, MA: Charlesbridge.

Keene, E. O., & Zimmermann, S. (1997). *Mosaic of thought: Teaching comprehension in a reader's workshop*. Portsmouth, NH: Heinemann.

The Kids' Book of the 50 Great States. (1998). New York: Scholastic.

Laminack, L. (1998). *The sunsets of Miss Olivia Wiggins*. Atlanta, GA: Peachtree Publishers.

Levin, J. R., & Divine-Hawkins, P. (1974). Visual imagery as a prose-learning process. *Journal of Reading Behavior, 6*, 23–30.

Louie, A. (1982). *Yeh-shen: A Cinderella story from China*. New York: Philomel Books.

Lowry, L. (1989). *Number the stars*. New York: Bantam Doubleday Dell Books for Young Readers.

Lum, D. (1994). *The golden slipper: A Vietnamese legend*. Mahwah, NJ: Troll Associates.

MacGill-Callahan, S. (1991). *And still the turtle watched*. New York: Dial Books for Young Readers.

Martin, R. (1992). *The rough-face girl*. New York: Putnam Juvenile.

Murrell, K. (2000) *Eyewitness: Russia*. New York: DK Publishing.

National Institute of Child Health and Human Development. (2000). *Report of the National Reading Panel. Teaching children to read: An evidence-based assessment of the scientific research literature on reading and its implications for reading instruction* (NIH Publication No. 00-4769). Washington, DC: U.S. Government Printing Office.

National Institute for Literacy (2007) http://www.nifl.gov/ partnershipforreading/explore/fluency.html

National Reading Panel Report. (2000). Bethesda, MD: National Reading Panel.

Nielsen, N. J. (2000). *Lia's journey*. Glenview, IL: Addison-Wesley Educational Publishers, Inc.

Novak, J. D. (1991). Clarify with concept maps. *The Science Teacher, 587*(7), 45–49.

O'Dell, S. (1960). *Island of the blue dolphins*. New York: Dell Yearling.

Osborne, M. P. (2002). *New York's bravest*. New York: Alfred A. Knopf.

Pearson, P. D., & Duke, N. K. (2002). Chapter 10: Effective practices for developing reading comprehension. In *What research has to say about reading instruction* (3rd ed.). Newark, DE: International Reading Association.

Pearson, P. D., & Gallagher, M. C. (1983). The instruction of reading comprehension. *Contemporary Educational Psychology, 8*, 317–344. Perrault, C. (1954). *Cinderella*. New York: Scribner.

Philbrick, R. (2001). *Freak the mighty*. New York: Scholastic Paperbacks. Pinnell, G. S., Pikulski, J. J., Wixson, K.K., Campbell, J. R., Gough, P. B., & Beatty, A. S. (1995). *Listening to children read aloud*. Washington, DC: U.S. Department of Education, National Center for Education Statistics,

Pressley, M., Wharton-McDonald, R., Mistretta-Hampston, J., & Echevarria, M. (1998). Literacy instruction in 10 fourth- and fifth-grade classrooms in upstate New York. *Scientific Studies of Reading, 2*, 159–194.

Rasinski, T. V. (2003). *The fluent reader.* New York: Scholastic.

Russell, S. A. (2000). *Year of the Ojibwa.* Glenview, IL: Addison-Wesley Educational Publishers, Inc.

Ryan, P. M. (2000). *When Marian sang.* New York: Scholastic.

Rylant, C. (1985). *The relatives came.* New York: Simon & Schuster Books for Young Readers.

Sachar, L. (1998). *Holes.* New York: Farrar, Straus and Giroux.

San Souci, R. D. (1998). *Cendrillon: A Caribbean Cinderella.* New York: Simon & Schuster Books for Young Readers.

Silverstein, S. (1981). *A light in the attic.* New York: HarperCollins Children's Books.

Steptoe, J. (1987). *Mufaro's beautiful daughters: An African tale.* New York: Amistad.

Stewart, S. (2001). *The journey.* New York: Farrar, Straus and Giroux.

Terban, M. (1983). *In a pickle and other funny idioms.* New York: Clarion Books.

Terban, M. (1990). *Punching the clock: Funny action idioms.* New York: Clarion Books.

Tovani, C. (2000). *I read it, but I don't get it: Comprehension strategies for adolescent readers.* Portland, ME: Stenhouse Publishers.

Trelease, J. (2006) *The read-aloud handbook* (6th ed.). New York: Penguin Group.

Triefeldt Studios, Inc. (2006, December 29). World of wonder: Snowflakes, in *The State,* Columbia, SC.

Truss, L. (2006). *Eats, shoots and leaves: Why commas really do make a difference.* New York: Putnam Juvenile.

Wenglinsky, H. (2004). Facts or critical thinking skills? What NAEP results say. *Educational Leadership, 62*(1), 8–12.

Woodruff, E. (1999). *The memory coat.* New York: Scholastic.

Yolen, J. (1992). *Encounter.* New York: Harcourt Children's Books.

Young, E. *What about me?* (2002). New York: Philomel Books.

Cited and Other Suggested Songs

"Gone Country" by Alan Jackson (Record label: Arista; released June 28, 1994)

"Suds in the Bucket" by Sara Evans (Record label: RCA; released August 19, 2003)

"That's What I Love About Sunday" by Craig Morgan (Record label: Broken Bow; released March 8, 2005)

"We Are Family" by Sister Sledge (Record label: Rhino/Wea; released June 20, 1995)

Additional Web sites

www.allwords.com

www.behindthename.com

www.doe.state.in.us

www.eyeintheear.com

home.inreach.com/kumbach/velcro.html (article on California's Velcro crop)

www.indianastandardsresources.org/files/eng/ca_ela_6_1_2_a.pdf

www.librivox.org

www.timeforkids.com

www.wisdomquotes.com/cat_questions.html (quote on Sam Keen)

zapatopi.net/treeoctopus.html (article on saving the Northwest Tree Octopus)

SCHOLASTIC

From the Editors at Scholastic Teaching Resources

Dear Reader,

We're always delighted when teachers say, "Your books are the ones we use . . . the ones that go to school with us for a day's work . . . the ones that go home with us to help in planning. . . ."

Your comments tell us that our books work for you—supporting you in your daily planning and long-range goals, helping you bring fresh ideas into your classroom, and keeping you up to date with the latest trends in education. In fact, many Scholastic Teaching Resources are written by teachers, like you, who work in schools every day.

If through your teaching you have developed materials that you believe would help other PreK–8 teachers—help save them time, help engage their students, help enliven or enrich their teaching—please let us know! Send us a letter that includes your name, address, phone number, and the grade you teach; a table of contents for your book idea; and a sample chapter or activities to:

> Manuscript Editor
> Scholastic Teaching Resources
> 557 Broadway
> New York, NY 10012

Please understand that because of the large volume of interesting teacher ideas we receive, it will take several months before you hear from us.

Many thanks for all the work you do for children!

—The Editors

Teaching
Resources

Just-Right Comprehension Mini-Lessons

GRADES 4–6

As teachers, many of us have sat alongside children who can read all the words on a page correctly yet are unable to discuss what they've read because they didn't comprehend it. In this research-based book, Cheryl M. Sigmon and Lisa D. Gilpin share more than 50 mini-lessons they've designed to help children build the skills they need so they can comprehend what they read. Each lesson is linked to a National Reading Panel strategy, such as monitoring comprehension, generating and answering questions, creating and using images, summarizing, and more. The authors provide lessons for both fiction and nonfiction, and they also include ready-to-use graphic organizers and checklists.

Cheryl M. Sigmon currently trains and supports teachers in implementing the Four-Blocks® Model in schools throughout the United States and Europe. She has been a classroom teacher, a K–12 language arts consultant with the South Carolina Department of Education, and has more than 25 years of experience in the education field. She is the author of several professional books on reading and writing, including *Just-Right Writing Lessons Grade 4–6*, which she coauthored with Sylvia M. Ford. Cheryl and her husband, Ray, live in Columbia, South Carolina, and spend their spare time with their three daughters and two grandchildren.

Lisa D. Gilpin is a sixth-grade teacher at Sand Creek Elementary in North Vernon, Indiana. She has 10 years of teaching experience and has taught first, second, and sixth grades. Lisa also provides training and support for teachers throughout the United States in the area of balanced literacy. She and her husband, Bryan, live in Versailles, Indiana, and spend their spare time playing with their two dogs.

Teaching Resources

$18.99 U.S.
SC-989906

ISBN-13: 978-0-439-89906-2
ISBN-10: 0-439-89906-0

51899

9 780439 899062

SCHOLASTIC
The Most Trusted Name In Learning®

www.scholastic.com